上地流空手道

― 写真と解説で見る上地流の形 ―

Uechi-Ryu Karate-Do

Eight Katas of Uechi-Ryu illustrated with photos and commentary

はじめに

　上地流空手道の形については、ビデオでいくつか出されている。しかし、八つのすべての形について、写真と日本語で解説した本はまだ出版されていない。

　上地流の形の解説書を出版したい、と考えている関係者は多いと思うが、ビデオのように簡単ではない。実に手間ひまがかかるのである。

　私は昭和59（1984）年以来フランスに住み、この国を中心に欧州で上地流の普及に携わっている。その間、形の本の出版について、幾度か話も出たし要望もあった。

　昼は銀行勤めをし、夜間に空手の指導をしていたので、本を制作する時間は簡単に取れなかった。

　さらには、平成12（2000）年以前はアナログ写真の時代であり、形の本を作るには、撮影し、現像し、写真を貼り付け、説明文を手書きする、という本当に時間のかかる時代であった。

　2000年代に入ってから、カメラもデジタルに変わった。さらに、パソコンという、実に便利な物が普及し、原稿の編集もパソコンの画面で簡単に出来るようになった。とは言いながらも、編集の基本においては、パソコンの専門知識が必要であり、時間も労力もかかる。

　形の撮影については、プロの写真家である弟子の一人が担当してくれた。一度の週末で八つの形の写真撮りをした。私はパリから新幹線で5時間もかかるトゥールーズへ撮影に出向いた。

　トゥールーズにはバンソンという私の弟子が上地流の道場を持っている。彼自身はエンジニアであり、彼の生徒でティエリというプロの写真家がいる。私がトゥールーズまで行けば、写真撮影が出来るとの誘いがあった。

　週末だけの撮影であったので、打ち合わせをする時間もなく、空手着に着替え、すぐに本番に入った。写真を撮りながら企画を進めた。後日に写真を見直し、取り直す余裕もなかった上、写真の組み合わせも、撮った写真だけでやらざるを得なかった。

　本来なら、本当に満足のいく形の本を作製するには、写真の撮り直しや編集のやり直し等かなりの時間と労力をつぎ込まねばならない。関係者がお互いに身近に住んでいて、いつでも問題に対応できる状況が望ましい。残念ながら、私達はこのような状況にはなかった。

　ただ、私にとって幸いであったのは、写真を撮った人も、編集した人も、トゥールーズの上地流クラブの有段者で、上地流の形を熟知していた事である。さらには私の息子もエンジニアであり、私のパソコンで不具合が発生すると手早く対処してくれた。

　この解説書が曲がりなりにも格好を付ける事が出来たのは、写真とITの専門家がいて、彼らが上地流をよく知っていたからである。

　本書で使用している写真は、フランスの生徒向けに出版した仏語版の一部である。十分に満足のいく写真の組み合わせではない。ただ写真は実にきれいに撮れている。フランスだけで用済みにするには、もったいないような気がしたので、日本語版も作り直す事にした。以前に出版した自書に加筆をし、形の解説書も一緒にした『上地流空手道 歴史と流儀と形』と、形の写真を中心とした本作『上地流空手道－写真と解説で見る上地流の形』の二冊を出版する事にした。上地流を志す人達の参考になれば幸いである。

　カタの表記については「型」あるいは「形」とすべきとの議論があるが、私は状況によって使い分けをすべきと思っている。例えば宗家が会員の意思統一のために教本を出版するのならば、「型の教本」であろうと思う。

　私自身は當山清幸先生、上原勇先生、上地完英先生にもご指導を頂いたが、最終的には宗家の完明三世に大きな影響を受け、宗家の「型」に近づこうと努力をした。それでもどこかで自分なりの理念や工夫が出ている。自分の理念や情念やリズムを入れて表現したのが「形」だと思っている。競技で「形」という表記を使用するのは、この理由であろう。この本に掲載したのは私なりのカタだと思い、「形」の表記を使用している。

　今回、収録された自分の写真を改めて見て愕然とした。技や体形を見て、形の本作製のために写真撮影をするのは、10年遅かったとの思いが強い。撮影した2007年6月初旬に私は65歳半になっている。

　家内の病死がその一年前にあり、悲嘆のどん底にあった。悲哀と練習不足が重なり、体重が6キロも落ちた。73キロあった体重が67キロになっていた。三戦（サンチン）の形の写真を見ながら、老骸をさらしてしまったとの後悔が立つ。

　特別気になるのは、私の顔付きが険しい事である。家内の病死から一年しか経っておらず、悲しみや虚しさが胸中にうっ積していた。写真は晴々としない私の顔を正直に写している。

　生徒達から写真撮影の話が出た時、思い立ったが吉日と、トゥールーズまで出かけた。しかし実際には写真収録に心の準備は出来ていなかった。形の本を出版するのであれば、写真収録には、気力も体力も充実し、円熟した40～

Forward

50代が望ましい。ただ人生ではすべての条件が上手くかみ合うのは難しい。私の場合も、形の出版については、早い時期から話があった。その内に、その内にと思っている間に、60歳半ばを越してしまった。

写真を見ながら、万全を尽くせ得なかったのは残念であるが、自分の至らない点は、将来、生徒達が頑張ってくれたらと願っている。また、本書を自分の反省材料にし、もう少し頑張らねばと心に期している。

晩年の當山清幸先生はたびたび、「歳を取ると、空手の稽古で残るのは形だけだね。形をつかう楽しみしか残らないよ」とお話しになっていた。私も空手と共に穏やかに老いて、無心に形をつかう自分を夢見ている。

日々鍛え、形を舞いつつ、老いゆかん。

Regarding the eight Katas of Uechi-Ryu, there are already several DVDs, but there are no books to complete these eight Katas. The reason is probably because of the technical difficulty to print a book of Katas although the IT technology is well improved nowadays.

Fortunately some of my students like, Thierry Vatelin, professional photographer, Vincent Britelle, IT engineer, Tsuyoshi Shimabukuro, IT engineer, and myself, a PC user could find the opportunity to collaborate to print this book of Katas. I must thank them for their collaboration and also to Guy Parmella, Uechi-Ryu practitioner and English Teacher who corrected my English texts.

I first printed this book of Uechi-Ryu Katas in French. The pictures are so beautiful, therefore, I would like to publish this book in English in Okinawa for those Karate-kas who like Okinawan Karate.

I began Uechi-Ryu with Sensei Seiko Toyama, but I did have some occasions to practice with other Senseis such as Isamu Uehara, Kanei Uechi and Kanmei Uechi. Although I decided to follow the Katas of Kanmei Uechi, the Third Soke of Uechi-Ryu, respecting the original Katas of Uechi-Ryu, I can honestly say that there may be a few differences in my Katas in detail. Therefore, I suggest using this book for reference but you should follow your teacher's instructions at the club.

When the pictures for this book were taken, I was 65 years old and only one year had passed after the death of my wife due to cancer, thus, I look like a very sad old man in all the pictures. I would like to recommend the younger men to prepare their book on Katas while still young.

Toyama Sensei often said to me, "Getting old, we lose our force, speed and stamina. Our body cannot resist for violent fighting like young men. The last pleasure of Karate shall be to practice the Katas." So, I also want to get old enjoying the play of Katas like Toyama Sensei. " 日々鍛え、形を舞いつつ、老いゆかん : Train ourselves every day, enjoy playing the Katas, let us get old peacefully. "

筆者、2007年

2017年6月吉日
上地流空手道協会
欧州支部　代表

島袋　幸信

Yukinobu SHIMABUKURO
Representative of Uechi-Ryu Karate Do Kyokai
in Europe, June 2017

もくじ Contents

- はじめに　Forward ……………………………………………………………… 2
- 上地流空手道略史　A Short History of Uechi-Ryu Karate-Do ……………… 5
- 三戦　SANCHIN ………………………………………………………………… 9
- 完子和　KANSHIWA …………………………………………………………… 17
- 完周　KANSHU ………………………………………………………………… 27
- 十戦　SEICHIN ………………………………………………………………… 39
- 十三　SEISAN …………………………………………………………………… 53
- 十六　SEIRYU …………………………………………………………………… 69
- 完戦　KANCHIN ………………………………………………………………… 81
- 三十六　SANSEIRYU …………………………………………………………… 95
- 終わりに　Post Script ………………………………………………………… 108

※9ページ～107ページの写真で、特に説明のないものは、正面から見たカットです。反対側の向正面から見たカットには  というマークを入れています。

向正面	Back front
演武者	Player
正面	Front

The pictures on the pages from 9 to 107, if not specially explained, are taken from the front. Those taken from the back front are marked with

上地流空手道略史
A Short History of Uechi-Ryu Karate-Do

上地流空手道の師父、周子和
Shu Shiwa, Teacher of Kanbun Uechi

　上地流は、パンガイヌーン（半硬軟）という中国拳法を基にして編み出された、空手道の一流派である。このパンガイヌーン拳法は、周子和（1874-1926）という師父が、中国の福建省福州市で指導していた。
　周子和は偉丈夫な豪力の師父であり、龍虎鶴の拳術に優れていたが、特に虎形拳という、虎の闘争の動きを模した拳技を最も得意としていた。また、周子和は道教の士で、福州市では書画家としても高名であった。

　Uechi-Ryu is one of the styles of Okinawan Karate, whose origin is a Chinese boxing named Pangainoon. This style was taught by Shu Shiwa(1874-1926) in Fuzhou City of Fujian Province of China. Shu Shiwa(Zhou Zihe in Chinese) was of a rich family, a Taoist, and a famous painter and calligrapher. He was a man of strong physique, an expert of martial techniques created from the movements of several animals such as the dragon, tiger and crane. He received Kanbun Uechi who arrived to Fuzhou, Fujian, China in 1897.

上地流空手道の開祖、上地完文
Kanbun Uechi, Founder of Uechi-Ryu Karate-Do

　上地流の開祖である上地完文（1877-1948）は、明治10年（1877）5月に沖縄県本部町伊豆味で生まれ、家は帰農した元士族であった。
　明治30年（1897）3月、20歳目前の時、徴兵忌避の理由と、同時に武術修業を志して、沖縄から清朝時代の中国に出国、福州市で周子和に師事した。
　上地完文は福州では拳法の修業と共に、漢方薬を学び、その行商で生計を立てた。10年に及ぶ激しい修行の後に、完文は師の周子和からパンガイヌーン拳法の免許を皆伝された。
　その後、師父の認可を受けて、福州市から約200キロ離れた南靖という町で道場を開き、パンガイヌーン拳法を3年間指導した。

　Kanbun Uechi(1877-1948) was born at Izumi Motobu in northern Okiwawa. He was the first son of Uechi family descended from Samurai, but adopted country life.
　For the reasons to avoid the Japanese conscription and to learn the Chinese culture and a Chinese martial art, he went to China, two months before his 20th birthday. He met Shu Shiwa and learned from him Pangainoon Kempo for 10 years. After 10 years hard training, he opened his dojo at Nanjing in Fujian Province with the advice of his teacher, Shu Shiwa.

完文は明治43年（1910）に中国から沖縄に帰ったが、大正13年（1924）に和歌山へ転居。パンガイヌーン拳法を、和歌山市の社宅で初めて指導したのは大正15年（1926）だった。

完文の長男である完英（かんえい）（1911‐1991）は、昭和2年（1927）、16歳の時に、就職のため沖縄から和歌山市在の父の元に移り、同時にパンガイヌーン拳法の修行も始めた。

父の下での厳しい修行の後、やがて二世を継承した完英は昭和12年から17年（1937‐1942）にかけて、大阪や兵庫県尼崎市で、道場を開き指導を行なった。昭和15年（1940）に兵庫県尼崎市で道場を開設し、同時に、この年をもってパンガイヌーン流空手術を上地流空手術に改称した。

名称を改めたのは、パンガイヌーンという言葉が、日本人には耳慣れないものであり、意味もわかりにくかったからと言われている。また、父完文が異国で長い歳月をかけ、多くの苦難に耐えて拳法を修行し、日本に導入した業績を長く後世に残したいという願いもあったと思われる。

昭和17年（1942）4月、完英は沖縄北部の名護に帰郷し、この町で一般に門戸を開き、上地流空手術を指導し始めた。

明治43年（1910）に、上地完文により福建省福州から持ち込まれた、パンガイヌーン拳法は、関西地方で上地流空手術に脱皮し、実に32年を経過して、沖縄の人々の面前に現れたわけである。

二世完英は、練習生達が上地流を順序立てて、わかりやすく学べるように工夫を加え、指導体系を確立した。上地流を近代空手に脱皮させ、沖縄の三大流派の一つに成長させて、世界各国に普及させた。

上地完英の虎の構え　1952年
Kanei Uechi, Tigar posture, 1952

Kanbun returned to Okinawa in February 1910 after living for 13 years in Fujian. He married in May 1910 and his first son, Kanei, was born on June 1911.

Kanei Uechi (1911-1991) joined his father at the age of 16, who was already at Wakayama for work. Kanei learned Pangainoon-Ryu Karate-Jutsu named by his father, and after 10 years hard training he succeeded his father as Second Generation Master of this style in Japan.

In 1940 Kanei changed Pangainoon-Ryu to Uechi-Ryu because Pangainoon had no meaning to the Japanese and he desired to honor his father who had introduced this martial art in Okinawa after having taken a long and unbelievable amount of effort to master it. He returned to Nago, Okinawa in 1942, and began Uechi-Ryu Karate in Okinawa for the first time.

Kanei changed Karate-Jutsu to Karate-Do in 1957. He created the exercises of warming-up, basic techniques, and some new Katas so that the beginners could learn this style easily. He spent his 80-years life developing Uechi-Ryu, and thus Uechi-Ryu Karate-Do is now found worldwide.

完明先生と長男・完尚　2009年
Kanmei Sensei and his first son, Kansho, 2009

　上地流宗家は不思議と男子運に恵まれている。平成3年（1991）に父完英の跡を継いだ三世完明（かんめい）（1941－2015）にも、完尚（1971－）、完司（1973－）、完友（1980－）という空手に秀でた三人の息子達がある。三人とも幼少期から祖父や父から上地流の厳しい指導を受けて成長している。学生時代にはそれぞれが空手の競技で活躍し、人一倍の武才と身体能力、柔和な人柄で周囲を魅了している。三世完明は上地流の道統を子息達に伝承する、という三世代目の役割を立派に果たしたのである。上地流宗家は現完尚四世を中心に兄弟達の結束が強いので、大きな発展と躍進が期待でき、宗家を中心に上地流のさらなる世界的興隆を確信するものである。

　Kanmei Uechi(1941-2015) succeeded his father Kanei who died in 1991.
　He has three sons, Kansho(1971-), Kanji(1973-) and Kanyu(1980-). They are all very strong fighter karate-kas. Kanmei is well recognized for his responsibility of raising his sons to take over the art of the Uechi family and thus performed his duties as the Third Generation Master of Uechi-Ryu Soke.
　Kansho, the first son of Kanmei, became the Fourth Generation Master of Uechi-Ryu Soke in 2015 when unfortunately his father died. This new generation has a very nice character and an excellent technique of Uechi-Ryu. The Uechi-Ryu Soke shall grow up remarkably with this new generation of three young Samurais.

當山清幸先生　2004年
Seiko Toyama Sensei, 2004

　當山清幸先生（1928－2009）は上地流創設者の最後の弟子であった。筆者が師事した1962年当時の先生は上半身の筋肉が見事に発達し、上地流空手家の特徴で、両腕の外小手の筋肉が大きく盛り上っていたので、まるでポパイみたいな体形だな、との印象を強く持ったものである。先生の性格は穏やかで、大変に話好きな人であった。「観衆を魅了するように形をつかえ」との先生の言葉が今でも忘れられない。

　Seiko Toyama (1928-2009) was the last student of Kanbun Uechi, the founder of Uechi-Ryu. Toyama Sensei accepted Yukinobu Shimabukuro to his Dojo in 1962, who had strong impression to his Sensei like Popeye because his arms were so big, developed like the arms of Popeye with Kote-kitae(arm- hardening), but having a very soft and tender character. I cannot forget the words of Toyama Sensei; that we should perform the Kata so as to fascinate the audience.

普天間の上地流総本部道場

Honbu Dojo of Uechi-Ryu Karate-do at Futenma, Okinawa, Japan

上地流宗家四世代目を背負う若侍達。向かって右から次男完司、長男完尚(現四世)、三男完友。2009年4月

Three young Samurais of Uchi-Ryu Soke, from right to left, Kanji, Kansho and Kanyu, April 2009　Kansho is now the Forth Generation Master of Uechi-Ryu since June 2016.

三戦（サンチン）　SANCHIN

* 印は極めを入れる
* Sign of impact

三戦における注意： 肩を丸く落とし、肩甲骨を出す。背中をまっすぐにし、あご、両肘、腹、尻を締め、両ひざを内側に締める。

Notice on Sanchin: Drop both shoulders. Keep your back straight. Bring in the chin, elbows and knees. Tighten abdomen.

1－結び立ち
1–Musubi–Dachi

2－「用意」の準備、拳を腰に引きながら、つま先を同時にわずかに開く
2–Prepare "Yooi". Pull up both fists to the waist by openning slightly outward both foot-fronts

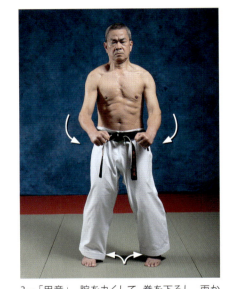

3－「用意」、腕を丸くして、拳を下ろし、両かかとを同時に開く、平行立ち
3–"Yooi" :Reach out both fists with the round form of arms. Open both heels together. Heiko–Dachi

4－両手を開く
4–Open both hands

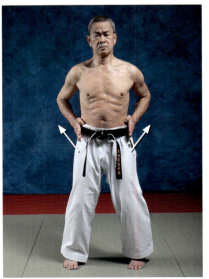

5－両手を腰まで引く
5–Pull back both hands to the waist

6－右足を踏み出す、三戦立ち
6–Put forward right foot by sliding

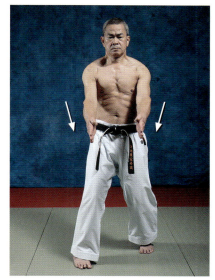
7―諸手抜き手、下方45° ✱
7–Both hands Nukite at 45° ✱

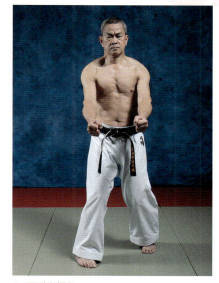
8―両手を握る
8–Grip both hands

9―三戦の構え
9–Open both hands, Sanchin–Kamae (pause)

●10〜13図の動作は三戦抜き手と呼ぶ。
●Pictures of 10 to 13, named Sanchin–Nukite. 10 to FIG. 13 operation is referred to as a three-round overhand.

10―三戦抜き手の初動
10–Begin Sanchin–Nukite

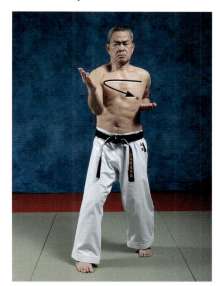
11―左の引き手
11–Pull back the left hand

12―三戦抜き手、手の甲を上にする ✱
12–Sanchin–Nukite, the palm down ✱

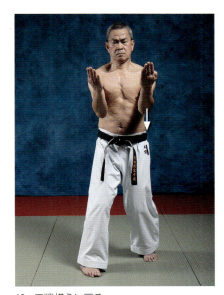
13―三戦構えに戻る
13–Pull back the hand, Sanchin–Kamae

14―左足を進める（左歩み足）
14–Slide forward the left foot

15―右手の三戦抜き手 ✱
15–Sanchin–Nukite with right hand ✱

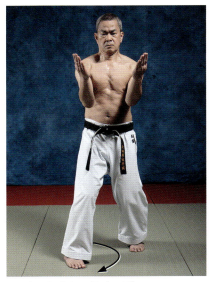

16ー右足を進める（右歩み足）
16–Slide forward of the right foot by sliding from inside to outside

17ー左の三戦抜き手
16図の三戦立ちから左手を右手に触れ、左脇に引き、まっすぐに抜き出す。手の甲が上になる。その後、三戦構え
17–Sanchin–Nukite ＊ Push the hand with the palm down, and Sanchin–Kamae (pause). Slide forward the left foot for next action

18ー左歩み足、その後に右三戦抜き手 ＊
10～18図までの左右の三戦抜き手を正面に4回、後ろに回転して4回、さらに正面に回転して3回行う
18–Sanchin–Ayumi(walk) and Sanchin–Nukite ＊ Do Sanchin–Nukite 4 times forward as shown by Pictures 10–18 , 4 times backward after turn, and 3 times forward after returning

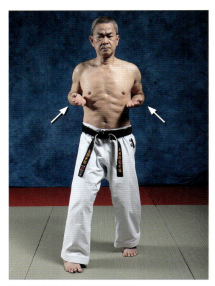

19ー三戦構えから両手を引く
19–Pull back both hands

20ー諸手抜き手、手の甲が上 ＊
20–Morote–Nukite (both hands), palms down ＊

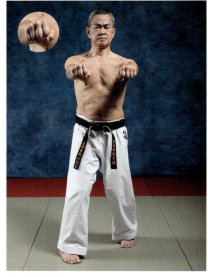

21ー手を握る
21–Grip both hands

三戦の呼吸法：胸式呼吸法であり、鼻からスッと短く吸い、口からシュと短く吐く。一般には動作の前に息を短く吸い、動作の後に息を短く吐く。腹部は常に筋肉を締め固めた状態にする。無理に息を長く止めない事。この形は中国福建省から上地完文により導入された。上地流において三戦はすべての形の基本であり、呼吸法と身体鍛錬のために不可欠な形である。

Sanchin Respiration: Chest breathing employed. Tighten abdomen constantly, short breathe in by nose and out through mouth. Generally breathe in before action and out after action. Don't keep your long breathe unnaturally. Sanchin was introduced by Kanbun Uechi from Fujian, China. Sanchin is the base for all Uechi–Ryu Katas and indispensable to learning Respiration and Body Hardening.

22－拳を返す
22–Turn both grips

23－拳を開く
23–Open hands

24－両手を脇に引く
24–Pull back both hands

25－諸手抜き手 ＊
三戦抜き手と同じく、手の甲は上になる
25–Morote–Nukite (both hands), palm down ＊

26－21〜25図 ＊ この諸手抜き手の動作を3回繰り返す
Same as Pictures of 21〜25 ＊ Repeat Morote–Nukite (both hands) 3 times

27－右90°に転進する。構えたままで右足で一歩進む
27–Sliding step by right front foot to right side 90°

● 28〜32図は輪受け（わうけ）と呼び、平手廻し受けと諸手の母指拳突きからなっている。
● Pictures 28-32 named Wa–Uke, consisted with Hirate–Mawashi–Uke and Morote–Boshiken–Zuki

28－輪受けの準備
28–Prepare Wa–Uke

29－平手廻し受け
29–Hirate–Mawashi–Uke

30－平手廻し受け
30–Hirate–Mawashi–Uke

31−右手は右腰、左手は左脇に引く
31−Pull back right hand to waist, and left hand to chest side

32−諸手の母指拳突き ✶
32−Boshiken−Zuki with both hands ✶

33−両手を引き、構える
33−Pull back both hands

34−左側に180°転進
34−Turn to left side 180° by sliding back foot

35−左側の輪受け、諸手母指拳突き ✶
35−Left hand Wa−Uke and Morote−Boshiken−Zuki ✶

36−両手を引き、構える
36−Pull back both hands

37−左側から正面へ転進
37−Slide step to front

38−輪受けの準備
38−Prepare Wa−Uke

39−平手廻し受け
39−Hirate−Mawashi−Uke

40－平手廻し受け
40–Hirate–Mawashi–Uke

41－右手を腰、左手を脇に引く
41–Right hand to waist, left to chest

42－諸手母指拳突き ✲
42–Boshiken–Zuki of both hands ✲

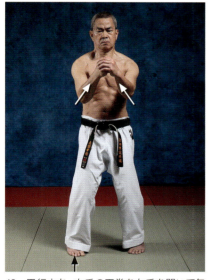

43－平行立ち、右手の正拳を左手を開いて包み込む
43–Heikou–Dachi, envelop right fist with left open hand

44－両かかとを同時に引き結ぶ
44–Join together both heels, Musubi–Dachi

45－礼
45–Rei

補足説明カット

● 13ページ27図～33図三戦の輪受け、14ページ34図の回転の仕方について補足する説明カットを掲載する。
● Picture 27~33 How to do Sanchin–Wa–Uke, Picture 34 How to turn.

27－三戦立ちと構え
27–Sanchin–Kamae

28－輪受けの準備
28–Prepare Wa–Uke

29－平手廻し受けを始める
29–Begin Hirate–Mawashi–Uke

30－平手廻し受け
30–Hirate–Mawashi–Uke

31－右手を右腰、左手を左脇
31–Right hand to waist, left to chest

32－諸手の母指拳突き ＊
32–Boshiken–Zuki of both hands ＊

33－引き手、構えを取る
33–Pull back both hands, Kamae

三戦立ち: 前足のかかとと後足のつま先が、一直線上に来る。前足は30°から45°の角度、後足はまっすぐに保つ。

Sanchin Dachi(Position): Keep on the same line the heel of front foot and the front of back foot. Turn inward the front foot to 30°-45°, and keep back foot straight.

34－回転の方法：後足のつま先を軸にかかとを内に捻る。体を回転させ、前足を後ろに置く
34–How to turn: Pivot on the front of back foot and slide the heel inside. Turn your body and put your front foot behind

後方への回転図：回転後も正確な三戦立ちをする事
Keep correct Sanchin posture after turning

三戦歩みの仕方: 三戦立ちから、前へ進むには、前足のつま先を軸にかかとを僅かに滑らせ、前足をまっすぐにする。その後で、後足を中心から外側に踏み込むようにして前へ進む。

How to do Sanchin Ayumi (walk): To step forward from Sanchin posture, slide slightly the heel of front foot on the axis of toes to keep the foot straight, and do slide–step of the back foot from inside to outside.

完子和（カンシワ）KANSHIWA

向正面から見た写真
The pictures shown from the back front

＊印は極めを入れる
＊Sign of impact

1－結び立ち
1–Musubi–Dachi

2－礼
2–Rei

3－「用意」の準備、拳を腰に引きながら、両つま先を同時にわずかに開く
3–Prepare "Yooi". Pull up both fists to the waist. Open slightly both feet outward

4－「用意」、腕を丸くして拳を下ろし、両かかとを同時に開く、平行立ち
4–"Yooi" : Reach out both fists with the round form of arms. Open both heels, Heiko–Dachi

5－構え
5–Kamae

6－左つま先を軸に左へ90°回転
6–Turn to left side 90° on axis of left tiptoe

7－右足を後ろに三戦立ち
7–Sanchin–Dachi on right foot back

8－正拳突きの準備
8–Prepare Seiken–Zuki

9－左手の平手廻し受け ＊
9–Hirate–Mawashi–Uke of left hand ＊

18

- 8〜25図は平手廻し受けと正拳の逆突き。左、右、正面に行う。回転はつま先を軸に行ない、転身の時点で素早く平手廻し受け。
- Pictures of 8〜25, Hirate–Mawashi–Uke and Seiken–Gyaku–Zuki, which shall be done to left, right and front. Turn on front of foot, perform Hirate–Mawashi–Uke and Gyaku–Zuki after turning.

10－右手の正拳突き ＊
10–Seike–Zuki with right hand ＊

11－引き手、構える
11–Hikite, and Kamae

12－右後足のつま先を軸に180°回転
12–Turn to right side 180° like Sanchin–Turn

13－左足を後ろに三戦立ち
13–Sanchin–Dachi with left foot back

14－左手の正拳突きの準備
14–Prepare left hand Seiken–Zuki

15－右手の平手廻し受け
15–Hirate–Mawashi–Uke of right hand

16－右手の平手廻し受け ＊
16–Hirate–Mawashi–Uke of right hand ＊

17－左手正拳突き ＊
17–Left hand Seiken–Zuki ＊

18－引き手、構える
18–Pull back hand (Hikite), Kamae

19－左足つま先を軸に正面へ向く
19–Turn to the front on left tiptoe

20－右足を後方に置き、三戦立ち
20–Left foot back, Sanchin–Dachi

21－右手の正拳突きを準備
21–Prepare right hand Seiken–Zuki

22－平手廻し受けの初動
22–Beginning Hirate–Mawashi–Uke

23－平手廻し受け ✶
23–Hirate–Mawshi–Uke ✶

24－右手正拳突き ✶
24–Right hand Seiken–Zuki ✶

25－引き手、構え
25–Pull back hand (Hiki–te), Kamae

26－右足三戦歩み、右斜めを向く
26–Right foot Sanchin–Ayumi (walk), face to right

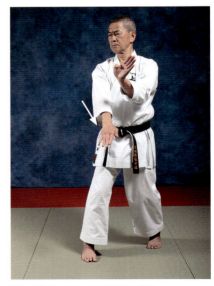
27－右斜めに向って平手廻し受け
27–Face to right and Hirate–Mawashi–Uke

28－右斜め平手廻し受け ✱
28–Right side Hirate–Mawashi–Uke ✱

29－右斜めへ足刀蹴り ✱
29–Yoko–Geri to right side ✱

30－左足三戦歩み、左斜めを向く
30–Left foot Sanchin–Ayumi, Face to left

31－左斜めに向って平手廻し受け
31–Face to left and Hirate–Mawashi–Uke

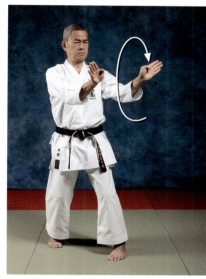

32－平手廻し受け ✱
32–Left hand Hirate–Mawashi–Uke ✱

33－左斜めへ足刀蹴り ✱
33–Yoko–Geri to left side ✱

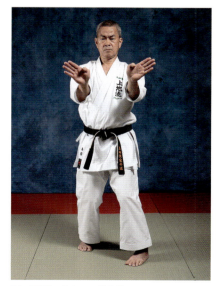

34－正面へ向かい、構える
34–Face to the front, and Kamae

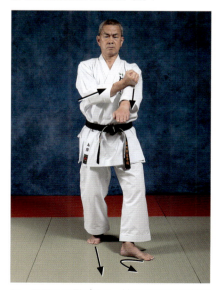

35－正面への飛び込み、前足のかかとを前に滑らせ、後足を踏み込む
35–Long forward step : slide heel of front foot slightely and do a quick slide inside with back foot

36－後屈立ちで平手廻し受け、右手は脇に引く ✱
36–Kokutsu–Dachi and Hirate–Mawashi–Uke, right hand Hikite on chest side ✱

37―横振り肘 ＊ 気合！
37–Yoko–Furi–Hiji ＊ Kiai！

38―縦裏拳打ち ＊
38–Tate–Uraken–Uchi ＊

39―後足のつま先を軸に後方回転
39–Turn backward on front of back foot

40―真後ろへ180°回転、三戦構え
40–Turn backward(180°), Sanchin–Kamae

41―40図を向正面から見る
41–Front view of Picture 40

42―輪受けを行なう
42–Begin the First Wa–Uke

43―左側の輪受け ＊
43–Left side Wa–Uke ＊

44―輪受けの後の母指拳突き
44–Prepare Boshiken–Zuki

45―寄り足して母指拳突き ＊
45–Yori–Ashi and Boshiken–Zuki ＊

22

46－引き手で構える
46–Hikite and Kamae

47－右足三戦歩み
47–Right foot Sanchin–Ayumi(walk)

48－二度目の輪受け
48–Second Wa–Uke

49－右側の 輪受け ✶
49–Right side Wa–Uke ✶

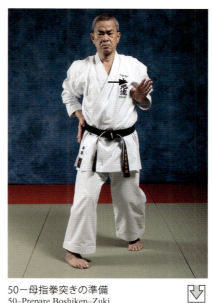
50－母指拳突きの準備
50–Prepare Boshiken–Zuki

51－諸手の母指拳突き ✶
51–Both hand Boshiken–Zuki ✶

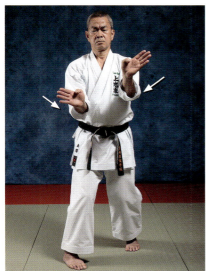
52－引き手で構える
52–Hikite and Kamae

53－3度目の輪受けと母指拳突き
47図～52図と同じ要領で行う
53–Third Boshiken–Zuki, repeat the same as pictures 47～52

54－右三戦歩み、手刀打ちの準備
54–Right foot Sanchin–Ayumi for Shuto–Uchi

55－左手の平手廻し受け ＊
55–Hirate–Mawashi–Uke of left hand ＊

56－手刀打ち ＊ 気合！
56–Shuto–Uchi ＊ Kiai !

57－裏拳打ちの準備
57–Prepare Uraken–Uchi

58－縦裏拳打ち ＊
58–Tate–Uraken–Uchi ＊

59－引き手で構える
59–Hikite, and Kamae

60－後足のつま先を軸に正面向きに回転
60–Turn to front as Sanchin–Turn

61－三戦立ちで構える
61–Put behind the front foot, Sanchin–Dachi, and Kamae

62－61図を正面から見る
62–Front view of 61

63－左手の平手廻し受け
63–Prepare Hirate–Mawasi–Uke of left hand

64－平手廻し受け ✱
64–Hirate–Mawashi–Uke ✱

65－前足の正面蹴り ✱
65–Left foot front kick ✱

66－引き足で構える
66–Hiki–Ashi Kamae

67－三戦立ちで構える
67–Sanchi–Dachi and Kamae

68－押さえ突きに移る
68–Prepare Osae–Zuki

69－寄り足しながら押さえる ✱ 押さえ突きの押さえは、平手廻し受けの要領で小さく廻して押さえる
69–Slide both feet and Osae–Uke ✱
Do a half size Mawashi–Uke for Osae–Uke

70－小拳（一本拳）突き ✱ 気合！
70–Shouken–Zuki (Ippon–Ken) ✱ Kiai !

71－後方へ寄り足で下がる。両手を小拳にして、両手の甲を重ねる。左手を外側に、右手を内側に重ねる
71–Slide back both feet together. Grip both hands in Shouken and bring them back to back with left fist outside and right fist inside touching

25

72－前足を引き、平行立ち
72–Pull back left foot, Heiko–Dachi

73－両かかとを引き合わせる結び立ち
73–Musubi–Dachi

74－礼
74–Rei

　完子和（カンシワ）は上地流の二番目の形で、初心者用の形である。上地流二世の上地完英先生が創作した。
　形の名前は、完文の完と周子和（しゅうしわ）の子和を採って名付けた。
　上地流の開祖である上地完文とその師父であった周子和の名前を、上地流を志す人達が心に銘記して欲しいとの願いで作られた形である。抜き手専用の福建拳法から握拳（正拳）を好む沖縄ティへの影響が僅かながら見える。

　Kanshiwa is the second Kata of Uechi–Ryu which was made for the beginners by Master Kanei Uechi, the second generation of Uechi–Ryu. This Kata was named with Kan for Kanbun and Shiwa for Shu Shiwa.
　Kanshiwa was made in the hope that all Uechi–Ryu practitioners would remember the name of Uechi Kanbun as Founder and the name of Shu Shiwa as Precursor. In this Kata we find some influence of Okinawa–Te which prefers Seiken to Nukite specialized by Fujian Kenpo.

三戦立ちの仕方
Sanchin–Dachi (Posture):

三戦歩みの仕方
How to do Sanchin–Ayumi (Walk):

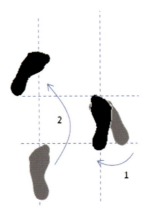

三戦立ちの足の位置と歩幅
1）後足のつま先と前足のかかとが一直線上に来る。
2）後足はまっすぐ、前足は４５°の角度。
3）両足の間隔は自分の肩幅程度にする。

Foot position and distance:
1) Put big toe of back foot on the same line as the heel of front foot.
2) Keep back foot straight and front foot at 45 degrees.
3) Keep the distance between both feet about the width of your shoulders.

三戦の歩み方
1）前足のつま先を軸にして、かかとを滑らせて、まっすぐにする。
2）後足を歩幅の中心から、すり足で外に踏み込む。

How to walk wih Sanchin Posture:
1) On the axis of the front of front foot, turn slightly the heel to straighten.
2) Firmly slide the back foot from inside to outside.

（注）昔は三戦（サンチン）の形における歩数と諸手抜き手の回数は一定していなかった。教師が生徒の体調を見て、回数を任意に定めていた。形の始めも、左右どちらの足を先に出すか、教師の指示があった。現在はほとんどの道場が団体演武をしやすくするために、始め方や回数に決まりを定めている。従って、各道場の方針に従うのが肝要である。

(Remarks)In the old days, the number of steps and that of Morote–Nukite (both hands) in Sanchin Kata was not determined. Teachers decided the number optionally by watching the physical condition of the student. Teachers instructed with which foot the students should begin. At present almost every club decides with which foot to begin and how many steps should be done. This decision might be taken in order to perform the group execution of Sanchin Kata. Therefore, it may be better to follow the rules of each club.

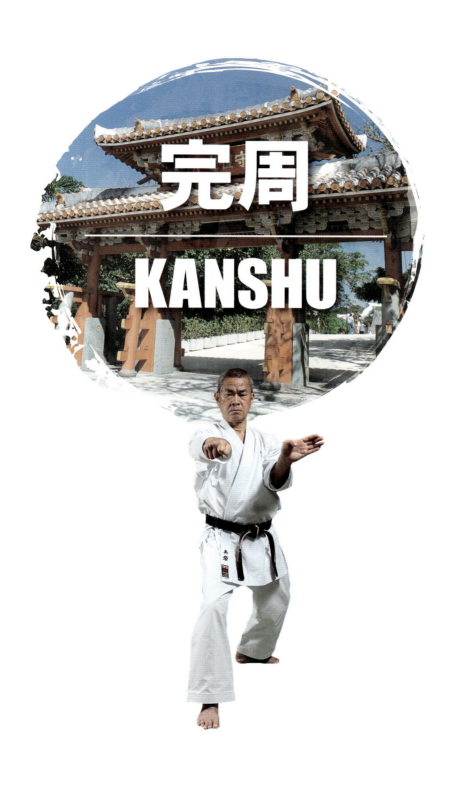

完周（カンシュウ） KANSHU

▽ 向正面から見た写真
The pictures shown from the back front

* 印は極めを入れる
* Sign of impact

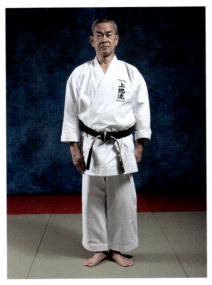
1−結び立ち
1−Musubi−Dachi

2−礼
2−Rei

3−「用意」の準備、三戦と同じ動き
3−Prepare "Yooi", like Sanchin

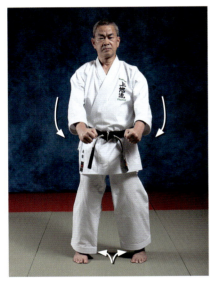
4−「用意」、三戦と同じ動き
4−"Yooi", like Sanchin

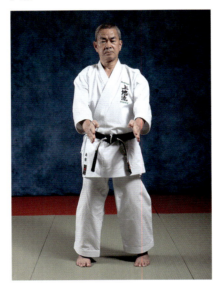
5−拳を開く
5−Open both hands

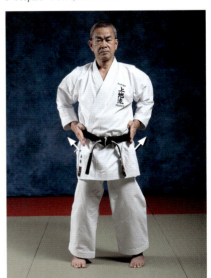
6−腰に引く
6−Pull back to waist

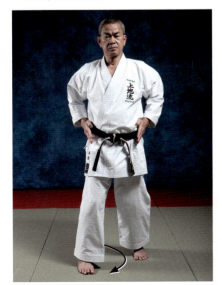
7−右足を踏み出す
7−Slide right foot forward

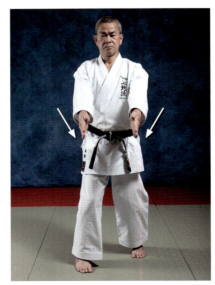
8−諸手抜き、45°下方 ＊
8−Both hands Nukite at 45° ＊

9−両手を握る
9−Both hands make fist

10−三戦の構えを取る
10−Sanchin−Kamae

11−三戦抜き手の初動
11−Begin Sanchin−Nukite

12−脇に引く
12− Pull to chest side

13−三戦抜き手、手の甲が上 ✳
13−Sanchin−Nukite, palm down ✳

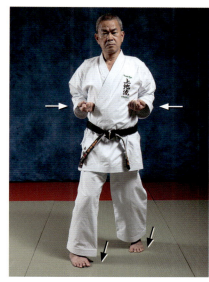
14−寄り足しながら小拳振り突きの初動
14− Slide forward and Shoken−Furi−Zuki

15−諸手の小拳振り突き ✳
15−Both hand Shoken−Furi−Zuki ✳

16−正拳かき分けの初動
16−Begin Seiken−Kakiwake

17−正拳かき分け受け ✳
17−Seiken−Kakiwake−Uke ✳

18−左手を開き、寄り足しながら縦裏拳打ち
18−Open left hand, slide forward with both feet and do Tate−Uraken−Uchi

19－縦裏拳打ち ✶
19–Tate–Uraken–Uchi ✶

20－引き手で構え
20–Pull back (Hikite), Kamae

21－右手を開く、左歩み足
21–Open right hand, slide step forward with left foot

22－左手の平手廻し受けの初動
22–Begin Hirate–Mawashi–Uke of left hand

23－平手廻し受け ✶
23–Full Hirate–Mawashi–Uke ✶

24－左前足の正面蹴り ✶
24–Mae–Geri of front left foot ✶

25－引き足で構える
25–Hiki–Ashi (Pull back the foot)

26－三戦立ちで構え
26–Sanchin–Dachi, Kamae

27－右足で歩み足
27–Slide step forward of right foot

28ー右手の平手廻し受けに移る
28–Begin Hirate–Mawashi–Uke of right hand

29ー平手廻し受け ＊
29–Full Hirate–Mawashi–Uke ＊

30ー右足の前足正面蹴り ＊
30–Mae–Geri of right front foot ＊

31ー引き足で構える
31–Hiki–Ashi (Pull back the foot)

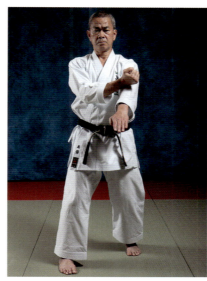
32ー三戦立ち、鉄槌に移る
32–Sanchin–Dachi, begin Tettsui

33ー左手の平手廻し受け、右手は鉄槌の準備 ＊
33–Hirate–Mawashi–Uke of left hand, and Tettsui with right hand ＊

34ー上段鉄槌打ち ＊ 気合！
34–Joudan Tettsui–Uchi ＊ Kiai！

35ー母指拳突きに移る
35–Prepare Boshiken–Zuki

36ー右手の平手廻し受け、母指拳の準備 ＊
36–Hirate–Mawashi–Uke of right hand, prepare Boshiken–Zukii ＊

37－上段への母指拳突き ✱
37–Joudan–Boshiken–Zuki ✱

38－母指拳の後に引き手
38–Hikite (pull back hand)

39－四本抜き手に移る
39–Prepare Yonhon–Nukite

40－左手の平手廻し受け ✱
40–Hirate–Mawashi–Uke of left hand ✱

41－右四本抜き手、手の平が上 ✱
41–Right hand Yonhon–Nukite, palm up ✱

42－引き手で構える
42–Hikite, Kamae

43－後足のつま先を軸に 後向きに180°回転
43–Turn backward 180° on front of back foot by sliding heel

44－後足が前、前足が後になる
44–Bring front foot behind

45－44図を正面から見る。三戦構えをする
45–Front view of Picture 44, Sanchin–Kamae after turning

46－三戦抜き手の初動
46–Begin Sanchin–Nukite

47－右平手を脇に引く
47–Pull back Right hand to chest side

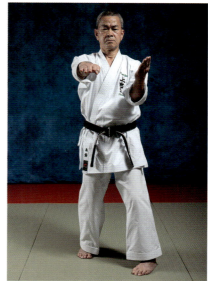
48－手の甲を上に抜き手 ✷
48–Sanchin–Nukite, palm down ✷

49－三戦の構えに戻る
49–Return to Sanchin–Kamae

50－一回目の四本抜き手に移る
50–Begin the first Yonhon–Nukite

51－寄り足で進み、平手廻し受け ✷
51–Yori–Ashi of both feet, Hirate–Mawashi–Uke ✷

52－右四本抜き手 ✷　手の甲が下
52–Right hand Yonhon–Nukite, palm up ✷

53－引き手、構え
53–Hikite, and Kamae

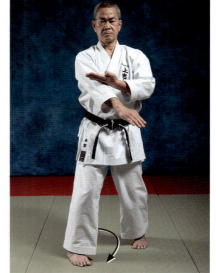
54－右歩み足、2回目の抜き手に移る
54–Right Sanchin–Step, begin second Yonhon–Nukite

55－右手の平手廻し受け ＊
55–Hirate–Mawashi–Uke of right hand ＊

56－左手で四本抜き手 ＊
56–Yonhon–Nukite of left hand ＊

57－引き手、構え
57–Hikite and Kamae

58－左歩み足、3回目の抜手準備
58–Left Sanchin–Step, begin third Nukite

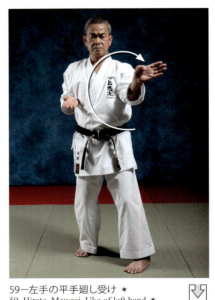
59－左手の平手廻し受け ＊
59–Hirate–Mawasi–Uke of left hand ＊

60－3回目の 四本抜き手 ＊
60–Third Yonhon–Nukite ＊

61－引き手、構え
61–Hikite and Kamae

62－左90°へ一歩転進、構え
62–Side step to left 90°, Kamae

63－左側の輪受け
63–Left side Wa–Uke

（注）三戦抜き手は手の甲が上になり、四本抜き手は手の甲が下になる。親指を曲げ、他の指四本を閉め、指をしっかり伸ばして突く。

(Notice)Nukite(open hand pick) : The palm shall be face down for Sanchin–Nukite and up for Yonhon–Nukite. Bend the thumb in, squeeze four fingers tightly together in the form of a spearhead.

64―輪受け ✱
64–Begin Wa–Uke ✱

65―左手は腰、右手は脇
65–Left hand on waist, right on chest

66―諸手母子拳突き ✱
66–Morote–Boshiken–Zuki(both hands) ✱

67―引き手、構え
67–Hikite and Kamae

68―右側へ右回りで180° 転進
68–Turn around(180°) by sliding

69―右へ寄り足で一歩転進
69–Slide both feet to backward

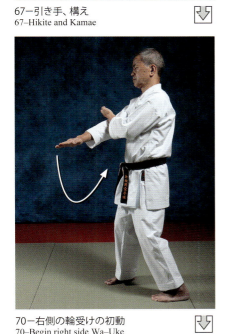
70―右側の輪受けの初動
70–Begin right side Wa–Uke

71―輪受け ✱
71–Wa–Uke ✱

72―右手を腰、左手を脇
72–Pull back right hand to waist and left hand to chest side

35

73―諸手母指拳突き ＊
73–Morote–Boshiken–Zuki ＊

74―引き手、構え
74–Hikite and Kamae

75―後足のつま先を軸に後転進、後足のかかとを内に滑らせる
75–Turn to left(back side) by sliding heel of left foot to inside

76―前右足を踏み込んで90°左へ転進、向正面に向かう、三戦立ち
76–Bring in right foot to backward

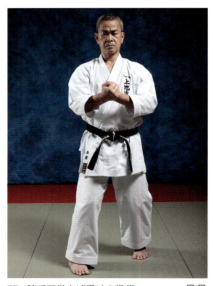
77―諸手正拳上げ受けの準備
77–Prepare both hands Seiken–Age–Uke

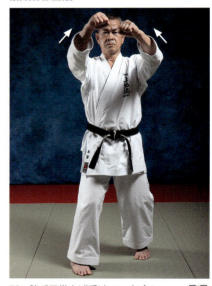
78―諸手正拳上げ受け ＊ 気合！
78–Both hands Seiken–Age–Uke ＊ Kiai !

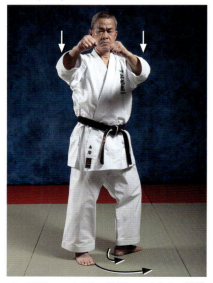
79―正面へ180°回転、後足のつま先を軸に回る
79–Hikite(Pull hands back), turn to the front as Sanchin–Turn

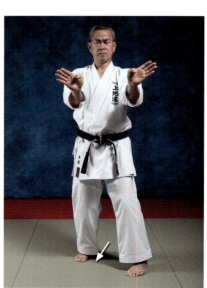
80―正面から見た図、左構え
80–View of the front, Hidari–Kamae(left posture)

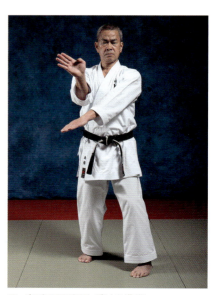
81―左手の平手廻し受けの準備
81–Prepare Hirate–Mawashi–Uke of left hand

82ー左手の平手廻し受け ✱
82–Full Hirate–Mawashi–Uke of left hand ✱

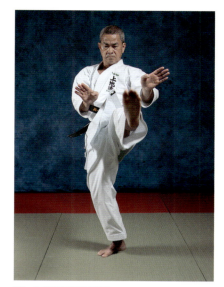

83ー左前足で正面蹴り ✱
83–Mae–Geri of left front foot ✱

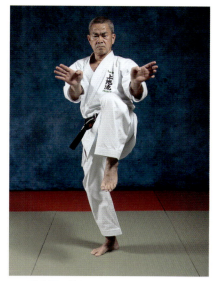

84ー引き足で構える
84–Hiki–Ashi and Kamae

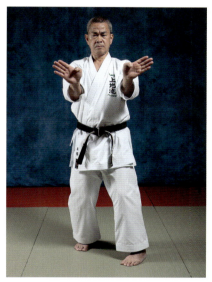

85ー三戦立ちで構え
85–Sanchin–Dachi Kamae

86ー踏み込みの準備
86–Begin Fumi–Komi (long step)

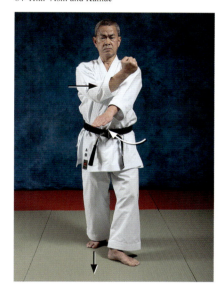

87ー踏み込み、横振り肘の準備
87–Prepare Fumi–Komi and Yoko–Hijji

88ー踏み込みながら、平手廻し受け ✱
88– ✱ Slide forward of back foot, Left hand Hirate–Mawashi–Uke to prepare Yoko–Hiji–Uchi

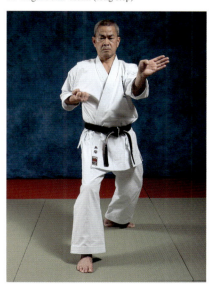

89ー後屈立ちで構える
89–Kamae by Kokutsu–Dachi, pull back right fist to chest side

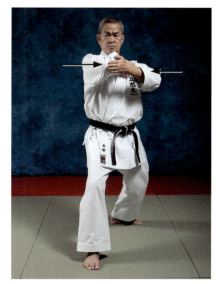

90ー横振り肘 ✱ 気合！
90–Yoko–Furi–Hiji–Uchi ✱ Kiai !

91―縦裏拳打ち ＊
91–Tate–Uraken–Uchi ＊

92―小拳（一本拳）に移る
92–Prepare Shoken–Zuki(Ipponken)

93―小拳（一本拳）突き ＊　気合！
93–Shoken–Zuki ＊ Kiai！

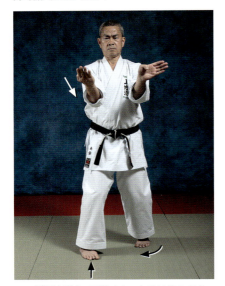

94―前足を引き、三戦立ち、左手はそのまま、小拳を開く
94–Pull front foot back for Sanchin–Dachi, open right hand

95―平行立ち
95–Heiko–Dachi

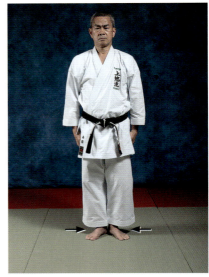

96―結び立ち、両かかとを同時に合わせる
96–Musubi–Dachi

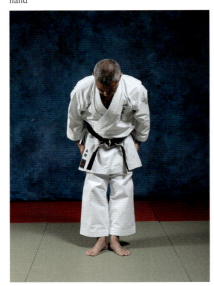

97―礼
97–Rei

　完周（カンシュウ）は上地流の三番目の形で、上地完英先生の弟子であった糸数盛喜先生（1915－2006）が創作した。
　この形は1960年代末までは、第二セイサンと呼ばれていた。セイサンを習う前の初心者用に創案されたからである。
　1970年に完周に改名された。完文の完と周子和の周を採り命名された。
　完子和の形と同じく、上地流の始祖開祖を追慕して名付けられた。

　Kanshu is the third Kata of Uechi–Ryu, Which was created by Seiki Itokazu(1915–2006) who was a student of Kanei Uechi.
　Kanshu was called Daini–Seisan until the end of 1960's because this Kata was created for the beginner to easily learn the Kata of Seisan.
　The name of Daini–Seisan was changed to Kanshu in 1970 by adopting Kan for Kanbun and Shu for Shu Shiwa in order to appreciate the memory of the Precursor and Founder of Uechi–Ryu Karate–Do, just like Kanshiwa which was named for the purpose of remembering these two great masters.

十戦
SEICHIN

十戦（セイチン）SEICHIN

向正面から見た写真
The pictures shown from the back front

* 印は極めを入れる
* Sign of impact

1−結び立ち
1–Musubi–Dachi

2−礼
2–Rei

3−「用意」の準備、三戦と同じ動き
3–Begin "Yooi" as Sanchin

4−「用意」、三戦と同じ動き
4–"Yooi" in same way as Sanchin

5−三戦立ちで構える
5–Sanchin–Dachi, Kamae

6−右手平拳上げ受けの初動
6–Begin right hand Hiraken–Age–Uke

7−右手平拳上げ受け ＊
7–Right hand Hiraken–Age–Uke ＊

8−中段平拳突きに移る
8–Prepare Hiraken–Chudan–Zuki

9−中段平拳突き ＊
9–Hiraken–Chudan–Zuki ＊

10ー平手構えに移る
10–Hikite and Open–Hand Kamae

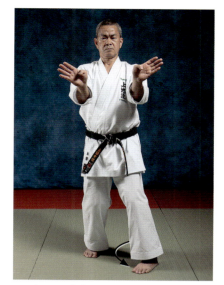
11ー左足、三戦歩み
11–Left foot Sanchin–Ayumi

12ー左手平拳上げ受けの初動
12–Begin left hand Hiraken–Age–Uke

13ー左手平拳上げ受け ✱
13–Left hand Hiraken–Age–Uke ✱

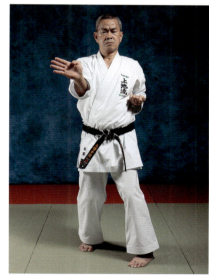
14ー中段平拳突きに移る
14–Prepare Chudan–Hiraken–Zuki

15ー左手中段平拳突き ✱
15–Left hand HIraken–Chudani–Zuki ✱

16ー平手構えに移る
16–Hikite and open–hand Kamae

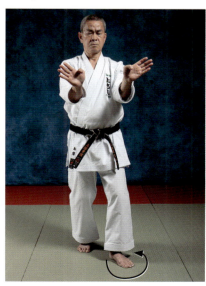
17ー左45°へ転進、左つま先を軸にする
17–Turn to left 45° on front of left front foot

18ー三戦立ち、後足を移す
18–Move back foot behind and Sanchin–Dachi Kamae

41

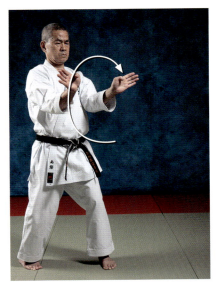
19ー左手の平手廻し受け ＊
19–Hirate–Mawashi–Uke of left front hand ＊

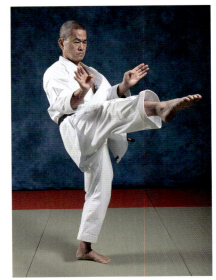
20ー右後足前蹴り ＊
20–Mae–Geri of right back foot ＊

21ー引き足
21–Hiki–Ashi

22ー構えに戻る、三戦立ち
22ーSanchin–Dachi and Kamae

23ー右正面45°へ転進、右後足のつま先を軸に回転する
23–Turn to Right side 45° of front, turn on front of right back foot

24ー左足を移す、三戦立ちで構える
24–Move left foot to back, and Sanchin–Dachi Kamae

25ー右手の平手廻し受け ＊
25–Hirate–Mawashi–Uke of right hand ＊

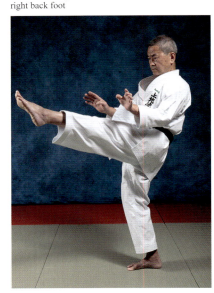
26ー左後足前蹴り ＊
26–Mae–Geri of left back foot ＊

27ー引き足
27–Hiki–Ashi and Kamae

28－構え、三戦立ち
28–Sanchi–Dachi and Kamae

29－正面に向かう、つま先を軸にして転進
29–Face to front , turn on front of both feet on the spot

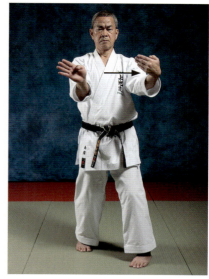

30－左手で横へ中段手甲拳受け ✻
30–Left hand Shukou–Ken–Uke against a Chudan–Zuki ✻

31－手を返して、相手の拳を掴む
31–Turn the hand to grab

32－相手の拳を包み込むように押さえて掴む ✻
32–Grab the wrist ✻

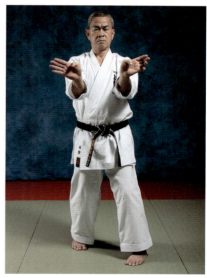

33－構え、三戦立ち
33–Sanchin–Dachi and Kamae

34－右足三戦歩み、右手中段甲拳受け ✻
34–Sanchin–Ayumi and Shukou–Ken–Uke against Chudan–Zuki ✻

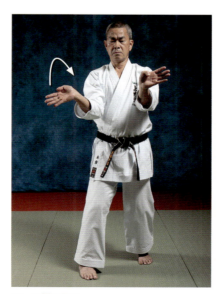

35－31図に同じ
35–Turn the hand to grab.

36－32図に同じ ✻
36–Grab the wrist ✻

37ー構え、三戦立ち
37–Sanchin–Dachi and Kamae

38ー真後ろへ回転する
38–Turn to the back

39ー向正面から見た図
39–Front view of the back, begin Kakiwake–Uke

40ー正拳かき分け受け
40–Seiken–Kakiwake–Uke

41ー平手にして腰へ引く
41–Open both hands and pull back to waist

42ー寄り足しながら45°下方へ抜き手 ✱
42–Yori–Ashi and Morote–Nukite at 45° down ✱

43ー両手で掴む、小拳の形、落ち上げて、左へ移す
43–Grab with both hands in form of Shoken, and pull up

44ー後足のつま先を軸に左へ転進、両手小拳、三戦立ち
44–Turn to left 90° pulling up both hands with Shoken, Sanchin–Dachi

45ー踏み込み、振り肘の初動、前足のつま先を軸に飛び込む
45–Prepare a long slide step forward

46―後屈立ち、左手廻受け ∗
46–Left hand Mawashi–Uke, Kokutsu–Dachi ∗

47―振り肘　気合！
47–Furihiji–Ate ∗ Kiai !

48―後足のつま先を軸に三戦立ちに戻る
48–Return to Sanchin–Dachi on the back foot

49―右手の平手廻し受け ∗
49–Hirate–Mawashi–Uke of right hand ∗

50―左母指拳突き ∗
50–Left hand Boshiken–Zuki ∗

51―右四本抜き手の準備
51–Prepare right hand Yonhon–Nukite

52―左手の平手廻し受け ∗
52–Hirate–Mawashi–Uke of left hand ∗

53―右四本抜き手 ∗
53–Right hand Yonhon–Nukite ∗

54―引き手、構え
54–Hikite and Kamae

55―右へ180°の回転、後足のつま先を軸に回転
55–Turn to right 180° like Sanchin–Turn

56―前足を後ろに移して、三戦立ちになる
56–Move Front foot to back Sanchin–Dachi, Kamae

57―左前足の正面蹴り
57–Prepare Mae–Geri by Front Foot

58―左手の平手廻し受け ＊
58–Hirate–Mawashi–Uke of left hand ＊

59―左前足の正面蹴り ＊
59–Front Foot Mae–Geri ＊

60―引き足にして構え
60–Hiki–Ashi and Kamae

61―三戦立ちで構え
61–Sanchi–Dachi and Kamae

62―前足を軸に向正面90°へ転進
62–Turn to back side 90° on front of front foot

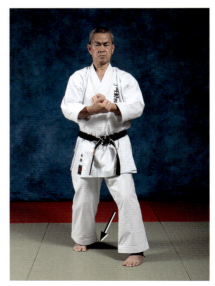

63―上げ受けに移る
63–Move back foot behind, prepare Age–Uke

46

64-諸手上げ受け ＊
64–Morote–Age–Uke(both hands) ＊

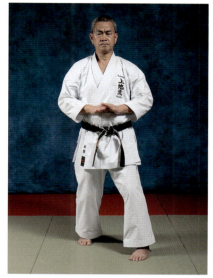
65-後足の膝蹴りに移る
65–Prepare Back Foot Hiza–Geri

66-前足を進めて、両手を重ねて抜き手をする
66–Small slide step by front foot and Nukite by both hands

67-平手かき分け、右膝蹴り ＊ 気合！
67–Hirate–Kakiwake and Hiza–Geri ＊ Kiai !

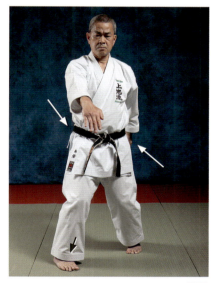
68-右足を下ろす、振り抜きに移る
68–Put down Right Foot for Sanchin–Dachi and prepare Furi–nuki

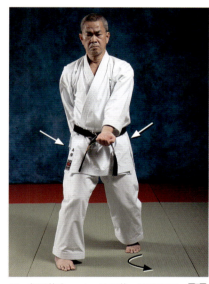
69-振り抜き ＊ その後 正面に回転する。後足のつま先を軸にして回る
69–Full Furi–Nuki and turn to Front with Sanchin–Turn ＊

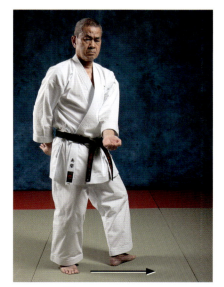
70-正面へ回転
70–Turn to the front as Sanchin

71-回転しながら振り抜き
71–Furi–Nuki by turning

72-振り抜き ＊ 正面から見る
72–Front view of Furi–Nuki ＊

73―平手廻し受けへ移る
73–Begin Hirate–Mawashi–Uke

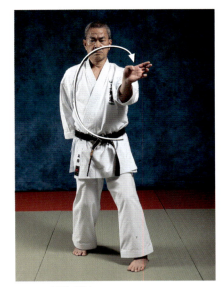

74―平手廻し受け ✶
74–Full Hirate–Mawashi–Uke ✶

75―後足のつま先を軸に左へ90°転進
75–Turn to left 90° on front of back foot, move left front foot

76―構え、三戦立ち
76–Sanchin–Dachi and Kamae

77―左平手下段払い、右手すくい受け、左膝受け、同時に行う
77–Left hand open Gedan–Barai, right hand Sukui–Uke, left foot Hiza–Uke

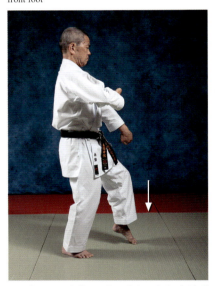

78―左平手下段払い、右手すくい受け、左膝受けを同時に終わる。猫足立ち
78–Begin the three actions and end them at same time, take Nekoashi–Dachi

79―三戦立ち構え、右へ180°回転、後足のつま先を軸にする
79–Return to Sanchin–Dachi, and to right side 180° by Sanchin–Turn

80―三戦立ち構え
80–Kamae, Sanchin–Dachi

81―77図に同じ、右手の下段払い、左手のすくい受け、右膝受け
81–Right hand Gedan–Barai, left hand Sukui–Uke, right foot Hiza–Uke, oposit of picture 77

82-78図に同じ、反対の手足で行う。猫足立ち ＊
82–Neko–Ashi–Dachi ＊

83-90°左へ回転し、正面に向かう、三戦構え
83–Turn to left 90° for front on the spot, Sanchin–Dachi Kamae

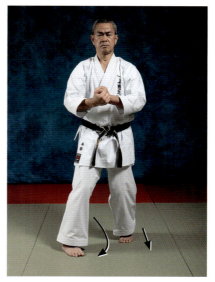
84-正面弾きに移る。後足前進
84–Begin Shomen–Hajiki, slide back foot first and front foot follows

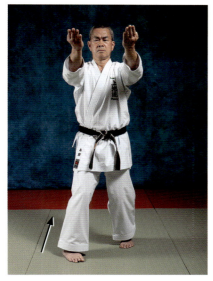
85-正面弾き ＊ 三戦立ち
85–Full Shomen–Hajiki, Sanchin–Dachi ＊

86-後方へ下がる。前足を引く
86–Slide back by pulling Front foot

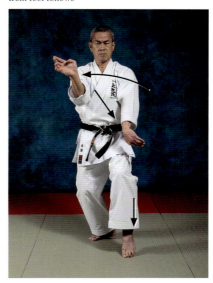
87-猫足立ちになる
87–Neko–Ashi–Dachi

88-横振り肘打ちへ移る
88–Prepare Yoko–Furihiji–Uchi

89-進みながら左手の平手廻し受け ＊
89–Long slide step and Hirate–Mawashi–Uke of left hand ＊

90-横振り肘 ＊ 気合！
90–Yoko Furi–Hiji–Ate ＊ Kiai !

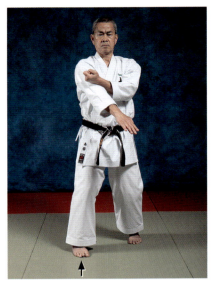
91－小拳突きに移る。三戦立ち
91–Sanchin–Dachi, prepare Shoken–Zuki

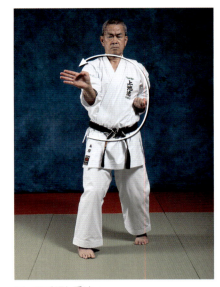
92－平手廻し受け ✱
92–Right hand full Hirate–Mawashi–Uke ✱

93－左、小拳突き ✱
93–Left hand full Shoken–Zuki ✱

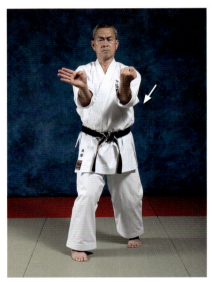
94－引き手
94–Hikite

95－右の小拳突きに移る
95–Prepare Right hand Shoken–Zuki

96－左手の平手廻し受け ✱
96–Hirate–Mawashi–Uke of left hand ✱

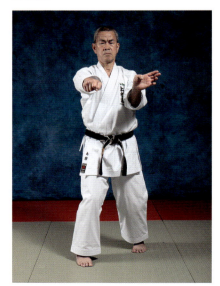
97－小拳突き ✱
97–Right hand Shoken–Zuki ✱

98－前足を引き、左手の平手廻し受け
98–Pull back front foot and Hirate–Mawashi–Uke of left hand

99－左手の平手廻し受け ✱
99–Hirate–Mawashi–Uke of left hand ✱

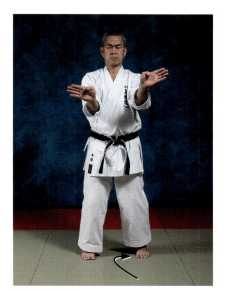

100―平行立ち
100–Heiko–Dachi

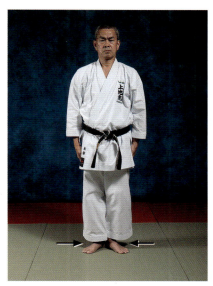

101―結び立ち
101–Musubi–Dachi

102―礼
102–Rei

　十戦（セイチン）の形は、上地完文先生の弟子であった上原三郎先生（1898－1966）が創作した。左右の手足が同じ技を練習できるようになっているのと、中国福建拳法の華麗な技を取り入れているのが、この形の特徴である。

　十戦は男子十歳の技量を意味する。男子十歳は、昔の沖縄では元服間近の年齢である。十戦を習う頃から、空手の恐ろしさ、面白さが分かって来る段階にある事を意味する。

Seichin Kata was created by Saburo Uehara (1898–1966) who was a student of Kanbun Uechi.

The comments of this Kata are: the right and left hands and feet can practice the same technique, and many splendid techniques of Fujian Kempo are employed.

Seichin means the ability of the boy aged 10 years old who has arrived near to the adult. In the old days of Okinawa the boys joined the category of adults when they became 13 years old. When Seichin has been learnt, we can recognize the dangers or the interests of Karate.

Sanchin means that we have reached the level to put aside our natural movements and adopt reasonable martial arts techniques.

補足説明カット

● 47ページ72図、48ページ76～78図、49ページ85～87図を補足する説明カットを掲載する。
● Picture 72 How to do Furi–Nuki, Picture 76~78 How to do Sukui–Uke, Picture 85~87.

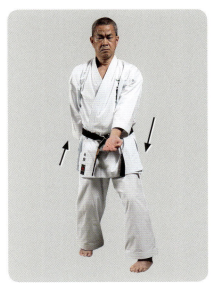

72―振り抜き　＊　正面から見る
72–Front view of Furi–Nuki　＊

振り抜き
Furi–Nuki

72図を横から見る
Side view of Picture 72

膝受け、平手下段払い、すくい受け―正面図76

76図を正面から見る。構え、三戦立ち
Front view of Picture 76, Sanchin-Dachi and Kamae

77図を正面から見る。左平手下段払い、右手すくい受け、左膝受けを同時に行う
Front view of Picture 77
Hiza–Uke by front left foot, Gedan–Barai by left hand and Sukui–Uke by right hand

78図を正面から見る。平手下段払い、すくい受け、膝受けを同時に終わる。猫足立ち
Front view of Picture 78.
Begin these three actions and finish at same time.
Neko–Ashi–Dachi Kamae

85図を正面から見る。正面弾き、三戦立ち ★
Shomen–Hajiki with both hands

86図　後ろ足で歩み足、ひざ受け
Slide step back of front foot, Hiza–Uke

87図　下段払い、小さく平手廻し受け、猫足立ち
Gedan–Barai, small Hirate–Mawashi–Uke and Neko–Ashi–Dachi

85図、86図、87図のポイント
　正面弾きの後に、右前足をすり足で大きく引いて下がり、左足で膝受けをし、左手で下段払い、右手で小さな平手廻し受けをする。下がった地点で、猫足立ちで構える。この四つの動作を同時に行うのが肝要である。

Points of Picture 85, 86, 87
　After Shomen–Hajiki, pull back right front foot with a long slide step back, do Hiza–Uke of left foot, Gedan–Barai of left hand and small Hirate–Mawashi–Uke of right hand. These four actions shall start and finish at the same time.

十三
SEISAN

十三（セイサン）SEISAN

向正面から見た写真
The pictures shown from the back front

* 印は極めを入れる
* Sign of impact

1－結び立ち
1–Musubi–Dachi

2－礼
2–Rei

3－「用意」の準備、三戦と同じ動き
3–Prepare "Yooi" in the same way as Sanchin

4－「用意」、三戦と同じ動き、平行立ち
4–"Yooi", Heiko–Dachi

5－抜き手にして腰へ構える
5–Pull back both hands to waist

6－左足を踏み出す、三戦立ち
6–Slide forward Left foot

7－諸手抜き手、下方45°　*
7–Both hands Nukite at 45°　*

8－拳を握る、正拳
8–Grip both hands to Seiken

9－三戦構え
9–Open both hands and Sanchin–Kamae

10－三戦抜き手を始める
10–Prepare Sanchin–Nukite

11－右手を脇にまっすぐ引く
11–Pull back Right hand to chest

12－抜き手、手の甲が上 ✱
12–Sanchin–Nukite, palm down ✱

13－引き手をし、三戦構え
13–Hikite and Sanchin–Kamae

14－右足、三戦歩み
14–Right foot Sanchin–Ayumi

15－左手の抜き手を始める
15–Prepare Left hand Nukite

16－脇にまっすぐに引く
16–Pull back to chest

17－三戦抜き手、手の甲が上 ✱
17–Left hand Sanchin–Nukite, palm down ✱

18－引き手、三戦の構えに戻る
18–Hikite and Sanchin–Kamae

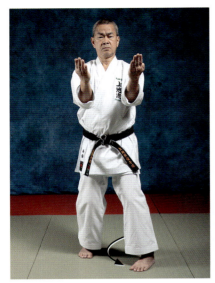
19ー左足、三戦歩み
19–Left foot Sanchin–Ayumi(walk)

20ー三戦抜き手を始める
20–Prepare Sanchin–Nukite

21ー脇にまっすぐ引く
21–Pull back to chest

22ー三戦抜き手、手の甲が上 ✱
22–Right hand Sanchin–Nukite, palm down ✱

23ー引き手、三戦の構えに戻る
23–Hikite and Sanchin–Kamae

24ー諸手背刀打ちに移る
24–Prepare Morote–Haito–Uchi(both hands)

25ー両手を胸元に引く
25–Pull back both hands

26ー寄り足、諸手背刀打ち ✱
26–By sliding both feet and Morote–Haito–Uchi ✱

27ー母指拳突きへ移る
27–Preparer Boshiken–Zuki

56

28―右母指拳突き ＊
28–Right hand Bosiken–Zuki ＊

29―左母指拳突き ＊
29–Left hand Boshiken–Zuki ＊

30―右母指拳突き ＊ 輪を描くように、3回行う
30–Right hand Boshiken–Zuki ＊ Do 3 times in circular movement

31―右膝蹴りへ移る
31–Prepare Hiza–Geri

32―左足を踏み込む、諸手抜き手
32–Slide step of front left foot and point with both hands Nukite

33―かき分け、右膝蹴り、気合！
33–Hirate–Kakiwake and Hiza–geri, Kiai !

34―振り抜きに移る
34–Prepare both hands Furi–Nuki

35―諸手振り抜き、左手が前 ＊
35–First both hands Furi–Nuki, left hand front ＊

36―180°真後ろへ回転、後足つま先を軸にかかとを回す
36–Turn baclward(180°) in the same way as Sanchin

57

37―回転しながら、振り抜き
37–Do Furi–Nuki while turning

38―振り抜きを決める ✽
38–Both hands Furi–Nuki ✽

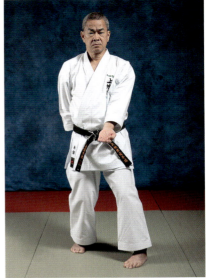
39―後ろへ回転後、向正面から見る
39–Back front view after turning to back

40―振り抜きの後、左手の平手廻し受け
40–Hirate–Mawasi–Uke of left hand after Furi–Nuki

41―平手廻し受け ✽
41–Hirate–Mawashi–Uke ✽

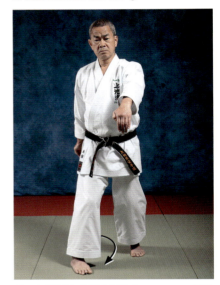
42―右歩み足、右手の振抜き
42–Right foot Sanchin–Dachi, right hand Furi–Nuki

43―振り抜き、右手が前 ✽
43–Second Furi–Nuki, Right hand front ✽

44―平手廻し受けに移る
44–Begin Hirate–Mawashi–Uke

45―平手廻し受け ✽
45–Hirate–Mawashi–Uke ✽

46－左歩み足、振抜きに移る
46–Left foot Sanchin–Ayumi and begin Furi–Nuki

47－3回目の振抜き、左手が前
47–Third both hands Furi–Nuki, Left hand front

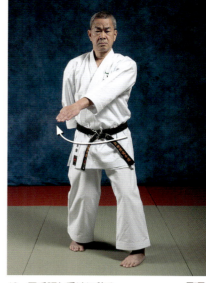

48－平手廻し受けに移る
48–Begin Hirate–Mawashi–Uke

49－左手の平手廻し受け ＊
49–Hirate–Mawashi–Uke of left hand ＊

50－下方への諸手抜き手に移る
50–Prepare both hands Nukite

51－寄り足前進、抜き手 ＊
51–Both hands Nukite to 45° doing Yori–Ashi with both feet ＊

52－相手を捕まえる、小拳
52–Grab with Shoken form

53－持上げ、右へ運ぶ。両足のつま先を軸に右へ90°回転
53–Pull up and move to right side 90° by turning on front of both feet

54－両手共に小拳の形、三戦立ち
54–Sanchin–Dachi, Shoken–Kamae of both hands

55－縦肘突きに移る
55–Prepare Tate–Hiji–Zuki

56－左手の平手廻し受け ＊
56–Hirate–Mawashi–Uke of left hand ＊

57－縦肘突き、前屈立ち ＊ 気合！
57–Tate–Hiji–Zuki on Zenkutsu–Dachi ＊ Kiai！

58－三戦立ちに戻る
58–Turn to Sanchi–Dachi, and prepare Bosi–Ken–Zuki

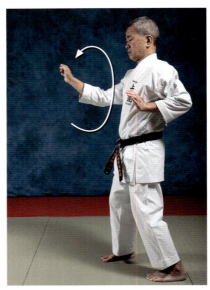
59－右手の平手廻し受け ＊
59–Hirate–Mawashi–Uke of right hand ＊

60－上段へ母指拳突き ＊
60–Left hand Jodan–Boshiken–Zukii ＊

61－右手の四本抜き手に移る
61–Prepare right hand Yonhon–Nukite

62－左手の平手廻し受け ＊
62–Hirate–Mawashi–Uke of left hand ＊

63－四本抜手 ＊ 手の平が上
63–Right hand Yonhon–Nukite, palm up ＊

64－引き手にして、構え
64–Hikite and Kamae

65－左へ90°回転（形の後方）、後足のつま先を軸にする
65–Turn to Left side 90°(back front) on front of back foot

66－右足を前に踏み込んで向正面に向かう
66–Slide step of right foot for facing to back side

67－右手の鉄槌打ちに移る
67–Prepare Right hand Tettsui–Uchi

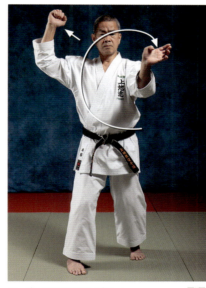

68－左手の平手廻し受け ＊
68–Hirate–Mawashi–Uke of left hand ＊

69－右鉄槌打ち ＊
69–Right hand Tettsui–Uchi ＊

70－母指拳突きに移る
70–Prepare Boshiken–Zuki

71－右手の平手廻し受け ＊
71–Hirate–Mawashi–Uke of right hand ＊

72－上段への母指拳突き ＊
72–Left hand Jodan–Boshiken–Zuki ＊

73－90°回転して右へ戻る。前足を移す
73–Turn to right side 90°(from back side) by moving right front foot by slide step

74－四本抜き手に移る
74–Prepare Yonhon–Nukite

75－右手の平手廻し受け ＊
75–Hirate–Mawashi–Uke of right hand ＊

76－四本抜き手 ＊
76–Left hand Yonhon–Nukite ＊

77－引手にして構える
77–Hikite and Kamae

78－左へ180°回転する
78–Turn to 180° side(left side) from back side

79－後足のつま先を軸に回転、前足を後方に移す
79–Turn in the same way as Sanchin

80－左前足の前蹴りに移る
80–Prepare Left front foot Mae–Geri

81－左手の平手廻し受け ＊
81–Hirate–Mawashi–Uke of left hand ＊

82ー左前足の前蹴り ✱
82–Mae–Geri by left front foot ✱

83ー引き足で構える
83–Hiki–Ashi and Kamae

84ー三戦立ちで構え
84–Sanchin–Dachi, Kamae

85ー右後足の膝蹴り ✱
85–Hiza–Geri of right knee ✱

86ー左手で頭を押える
86–Left open hand pushes down

87ー右手で小拳突き ✱　45° 下方
87–Right hand Shoken–Zuki at 45° ✱

88ー左手で小拳突き ✱（2回目）
88–2nd Shoken–Zuki of left hand ✱

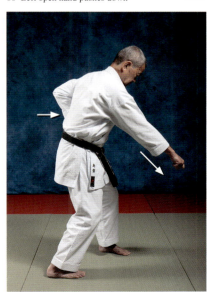
89ー右手で小拳突き ✱（3回目）
89–3rd Shoken–Zuki of right hand ✱

90ー三戦立ちの構えに戻る
90–Return to Sanchin–Dachi

63

91ーその場で三戦抜き手
91–Sanchin–Nukite on the spot

92ー三戦抜き手 ＊
92–Sanchin–Nukite ＊

93ー引き手で三戦構え
93–Hikite and Sanchin–Kamae

94ー右に90°転進（形の後方）、後足のつま先を軸に転進する
94–Turn to right side 90°(back front) on front of both feet

95ー左足をわずかに移動させ、三戦立ちになる
95–More slightly both feet on the spot to face to back front, Sanchin–Dachi Front view of back side

96ー三戦抜き手に移る
96–Prepare Sanchin–Nukite

97ー左手を脇に引く
97–Pull back left hand to chest

98ー三戦抜き手 ＊　手の甲が上
98–Sanchin–Nukite, palm down ＊

99ー引き手、三戦構え
99–Hikite and Sanchin–Kamae

100－正面へ回転、後足のつま先を軸に回転、前足を後に移す
100–Return to Front in same way as Sanchin–Turn

101－三戦の構え
101–Sanchin–Kamae

102－101図を正面から見る
102–Front view of Picture 101

103－その場で三戦抜手に移る
103–Prepare Sanchin–Nukite

104－脇に引き手
104–Pull back Right hand to chest

105－三戦抜き手 ＊ 手の甲が上
105–Full Sanchin–Nukite, palm down ＊

106－三戦の構えに戻る
106–Hikite and Sanchin–Kamae

107－右手の四本抜き手に移る
107–Prepare Right hand Yonhon–Nukite

108－寄り足前進、左手の平手廻し受け ＊
108–Yori–Ashi of both feet Hirate–Mawashi–Uke of left hand ＊

109-四本抜き手 ✳ (1回目)
109–1st Yonhon–Nukite ✳

110-引き手で構える
110–Hikite and Kamae

111-2回目の抜き手、右歩み足
111–Right foot Sanchin–Step for 2nd Nukite

112-右手の平手廻し受け ✳
112–Hirate–Mawashi–Uke of right hand ✳

113-左手を脇に引く
113–Pull back Left hand to chest

114-2回目の四本抜き手 ✳
114–2nd full Yonhon–Nukite ✳

115-引き手にして、構え
115–Hikite and Kamae

116-3回目の抜き手、左歩み足
116–Left foot Sanchin–Ayumi for 3rd Yonhon–Nukite

117-平手廻し受け ✳
117–Hirate–Mawashi–Uke ✳

118－3回目の四本抜き手 ✴
118–3rd Yonhon–Nukite ✴

119－引き手にして構える
119–Hikite and Kamae

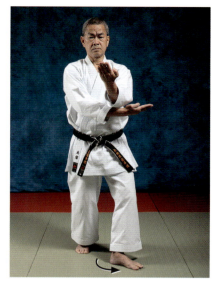

120－内受け構えに移る
120—Begin Uchi–Uke Kamae

121－後屈立ち、内受け構え
121–Koukutsu–Dachi and Uchi–Uke Kamae

122－後ろへ飛ぶ。後足を軸にし飛び上がって右前足を引く
122–Jump back on axis of back foot. Pull back Right front foot

123－その右足で後方に着地しながら、左足を上げる
123–Land with Right front foot on the back and pull up Left foot

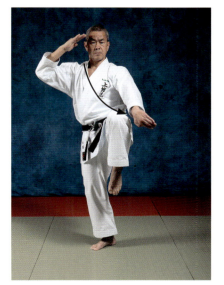

124－鶴足立ちの構え ✴
124–Tsuru–Ashi–Dachi Kamae ✴

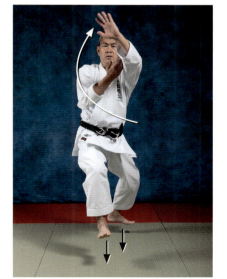

125－前へ飛ぶ、右足を前に、左足を後ろに引く、左手の平手廻し受け
125–Jump forward by crossing both feet and do Hirate–Mawashi–Uke of left hand

126－平手廻し受け ✴ 後屈立ち
126–Hirate–Mawashi–Uke by landing on Kokutsu–Dachi ✴

127－横振り肘打ち ＊ 後屈立ち、気合！
127–Yoko–Furihiji–Uchi ＊ Kiai！

128－縦裏拳打ち ＊
128–Tate–Urken–Uchi ＊

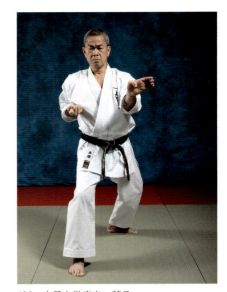
129－中段小拳突きへ移る
129–Begin Chudan–Shoken–Zuki

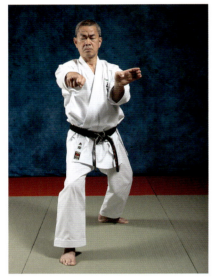
130－中段小拳突き ＊
130–Full Chudan–Shoken–Zuki ＊

131－拳を返す
131–Turn the fist

132－開きながら（抜き手の形）
132–Open hand like Yonhon–Nukite

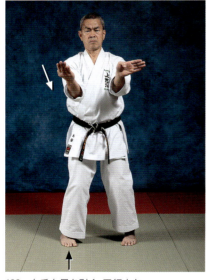
133－右手右足を引く、平行立ち
133–Pull back right hand and right foot. Heikou–Dachi

134－結び立ち、かかとを同時に引く
134–Pull both heels, Musubi–Dachi

135－礼
135–Rei

十三（セイサン）の形は、上地完文が中国福建省から導入した、原型そのものであると言われている。沖縄には昔、男児が十三歳になると、十三祝いという元服式のような祝いがあった。男児が十三歳になれば大人の仲間入りをしたのである。上地流では十三の形を習得した頃になると、黒帯の仲間入りという意味である。

The Kata, Seisan, was directly introduced by Kanbun Uechi from Fujian China in 1910 to Okinawa and is passed on to the present day without any changes. Seisan means 13 years old when the boy becomes adult in Okinawa. When we have learnt this Kata, we reach the level of black belt.

十六
SEIRYU

十六（セイリュウ）SEIRYU

向正面から見た写真
The pictures shown from the back front

* 印は極めを入れる
* Sign of impact

1―結び立ち
1–Musubi–Dachi

2―礼
2–Rei

3―「用意」の準備、三戦と同じ動き
3–Begin "Yooi", do as Sanchin

4―「用意」、三戦と同じ動き、平行立ち
4–"Yooi", Heikou–Dachi

5―右足を踏み出し、構える
5–Slide right foot, open hand, Kamae

6―諸手の上段上げ受けへ移る
6–Prepare both hands Jodan–Age–Uke

7―諸手の上段上げ受け
7–Morote–Jodan–Age–Uke

8―後方へ寄り足で下がりながら挟み受け
8–Slide back by Yori–Ashi and begin Hasami–Uke

9―中段の正拳挟み受け ＊　右腕を前にする
9–Chudan–Seiken–Hasami–Uke ＊　Right hand outside

70

10—縦裏拳に移る
10–Begin Tate–Uraken–Uchi, open left hand

11—縦裏拳打ち ＊ 気合！
11–Tate–Uraken–Uchi ＊ Kiai !

12—真後ろへ回転
12–Turn to the back as Sanchin

13—三戦立ち
13–Sanchin–Dachi

14—12図から13図へと180°回転後を向正面から見る
14–Front view after turn to back front 180°

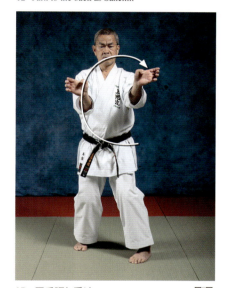

15—平手廻し受け ＊
15–Hirate–Mawashi–Uke ＊

16—前足で正面蹴り ＊
16–Mae–geri with left front foot ＊

17—引き足
17–Hikiashi

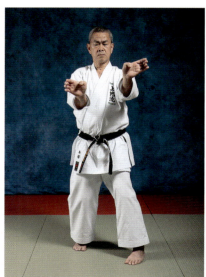

18—三戦立ちで構え
18–Sanchin–Dachi, Kamae

19ー押さえ突きに移る
19–Begin Osae–Zuki

20ー寄り足しながら押さえ受けをする ＊
20–Yori–Ashi and Osae–Uke ＊

21ー止まった時点で小拳突き ＊
21–Shoken–Zuki after Osae–Uke ＊

22ー寄り足で下がり、小拳の構え。左小拳の甲に右を重ねる
22–Yori–Ashi back of both feet and Shoken Kamae like Kanshiwa

23ーその場で90°右へ転進、両のつま先を軸に向きを変える
23–Turn to right side (90°) on front of both feet at the spot

24ー膝受けと輪受けに移る
24–Begin first Hiza–Uke and Wa–Uke

25ー膝受けと輪受け、24〜27図を同時に行う事
25–Bend and pull up right knee and do Wa–Uke at the same time(Picture 24-27 are serial actions at the same time)

26ー膝の下ろしと輪受けを同時に行う ＊
26–Finish putting down knee and Wa–Uke the same time ＊

27ー猫足立ちで構える、38図を参照 ＊
27–Kamae by Neko–Ashi–Dachi, see Picture 38 for Kamae

28－三戦立ちに戻る
28– Return to Sanchin–Dachi

29－左へ180°回転、後足のつま先を軸に回転する
29–Turn to left(180°) with Sanchin–Turn

30－三戦立ち構え
30–Sanchin–Dachi, Kamae

31－膝受け、輪受けに移る
31–Begin 2nd Wa–Uek and Hiza–Uke

32－膝受けと輪受けの初動作
32–Begin left Wa–Uke, Hiza–Uke

33－膝の下しと輪受け
33–Finish Wa–Uke and HizaUke

34－膝受けと輪受け、43図を参照
34–Do serial actions of pictures 32-33 at the same time, See Picture 43

35－向正面に向う。両つま先を軸に90°右へ転進する。三戦構え
35–Turn to right (back side–90°), Sanchin–Kamae

36－膝受け、輪受けに移る
36–Begin 3rd Wa–Uke and Hiza–Uke

37―膝の下しと輪受け ＊
37–Finish Wa–Uke and Hiza–Uke at the same time ＊

38―膝受け、輪受け、36―38図を同時に行う＊ 猫足立ち、構え
38–Do pictures 36-38 at the same time, Neko–Ashi–Dachi, Kamae

39―三戦立ちに戻る
39–Return to Sanchin–Dachi

40―正面に180°回転、後足つま先を軸にする
40–Return to the front 180° by Sanchin–Turn

41―三戦立ちで構え
41–Sanchin–Dachi, Kamae

42―4回目の膝受け、輪受けに移る
42–Front view, begin 4th Wa–Uke, Hiza–Uke

43―膝受け、輪受け、同時に行い、同時に終わる＊
43–Finish at the same time Wa–Uke and Hiza–Uke ＊

44―前方へ飛び込み、振り肘に移る。 後足を前方に滑らせる
44–Slide forward by doing Hirate-Mawashi–Uke to prepare Furi–Hiji

45―平手廻し受け、後屈立ち ＊
45–Hirate–Mawashi–Uke on Kokutsu–Dachi. Pull back left hand ＊

46―横振り肘 ＊ 後屈立ち、気合！
46–Yoko–Furi–Hiji on Koukutsu–Dachi ＊ Kiai !

47―縦裏拳打ち、及び小拳突き ＊
十三の129図と130図を参照
47–Tate–Uraken–Uchi and Shoken–Zui ＊ See Pictures 129/130 of Seisan

48―真後ろへ180°回転、後足のつま先を軸に回転
48–Turn to backward 180° on front of back foot

49―三戦立ちで構え
49–Sanchin–Dachi, Kamae

50―49図を正面から見る
50–Front view of Picture 49

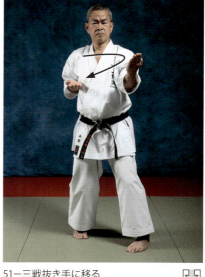

51―三戦抜き手に移る
51–Begin Sanchin–Nukite

52―三戦抜き手 ＊
52–Full Sanchin–Nukite ＊

53―腕を引き、構え
53–Pull back hand and Kamae

54―四本抜き手に移る
54–Prepare Yonhon–Nukite

55―寄り足、左手の平手廻し受け ★
55–Yori–Ashi by both feet and Hirate–Mawashi–Uke of left hand

56―1回目の四本抜き手 ★
56–1st right Yonhon–Nukite ★

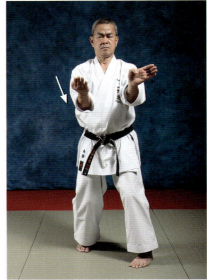

57―引き手をし、構え
57–Hikite and Kamae

58―2回目の抜き手に移る。右歩み足、右手の平手廻し受け
58–Prepare 2nd left Yonhon–Nukite, right foot Sanchin–Ayumi, Hirate–Mawashi–Uke of right hand

59―三戦歩み、右手の平手廻し受け ★
59–Sanchin–Ayumi and Hirate–Mawashi–Uke of right hand ★

60―2回目の四本抜き手 ★
60–2nd Yonhon–Nukite ★

61―引き手をし、構え
61–Hikite and Kamae

62―3回目の抜き手、左歩み足
62–Prepare 3rd Yonhon–Nukite, Left Ayumi–Ashi

63―左手の平手廻し受け ★
63–Sanchi–Ayumi and Hirate–Mawashi–Uke of left hand ★

64―3回目の四本抜き手 ✻
64–3rd Yonhon–Nukite ✻

65―引き手をし、構え
65–Hikite and Kamae

66―90°右へ転進、両足のつま先を軸に回転
66–Turn to right 90° on front of both feet at same spot

67―左手四本抜き手に移る
67–Prepare Left hand Yonhon–Nukite

68―右手の平手廻し受け ✻
68–Hirate–Mawashi–Uke of right hand ✻

69―左手四本抜き手 ✻
69–Left hand Yonhon–Nukite ✻

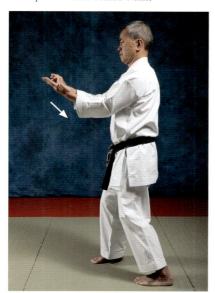
70―引手にして構える
70–Hikite and Kamae

71―左へ180°回転、後足のつま先を軸に回転
71–Turn to right 180° like Sanchin–Turn

72―三戦立ちで構える
72–Sanchin–Dachi, Kamae

73－右後足の正面蹴りに移る
73–"Prepare Mae–Geri of right back foot

74－左手の平手廻し受け ＊
74–Hirate–Mawashi–Uke of left hand ＊

75－右後足で正面蹴り ＊
75–Mae–Geri of right back foot ＊

76－引き足
76–Hiki–Ashi after Mae–Geri

77－後ろに足を置き、三戦構え
77–Replace right foot and Kamae

78－90° 右（形方向真後ろ）に回転する。両つま先を軸にかかとを滑らす
78–Return to the back on front 90° of both feet, and prepare Morote–Hajiki

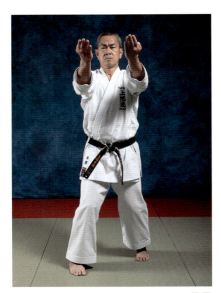

79－諸手で正面弾き ＊
79–Morote(both hand)Jodan–Hajiki or Jodan–Nukite ＊

80－形方向、180° 真正面に回転、後足のつま先を軸に回転
80–Return to the front 180° with Sanchin–Turn

81－80図を正面から見る。三戦立ちで構える
81–Front view of Picture 80, Kamae with Sanhin–Dachi

82−鉄槌打ちに移る
82–Prepare Tettsui–Uchi

83−左手の平手廻し受け ✱
83–Hirate–Mawashi–Uke of left hand ✱

84−鉄槌打ち ✱
84–Right hand Tettsui–Uchi ✱

85−左手の母指拳突きに移る
85–Prepare left hand Boshien–Zuji

86−右手の平手廻し受け ✱
86–Hirate–Mawashi–Uke of right hand ✱

87−左手の母指拳突き ✱
87–Left hand Jodan Boshiken–Zuki ✱

88−右手の四本抜き手に移る
88–Prepare right hand Yonhon–Nukite

89−左手の平手廻し受け ✱
89–Hirate–Mawashi–Uke of left hand ✱

90−右手の四本抜き手 ✱
90–Right hand Yonhon–Nukite ✱

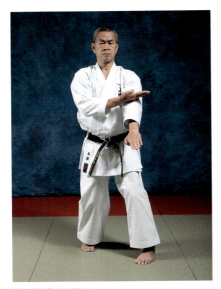
91―輪受けに移る
91–Prepare Wa–Uke

92―輪受け ＊
92–Wa–Uke ＊

93―諸手の母指拳突きに移る
93–Prepare Morote Boshiken–Zuki(both hands)

94―寄り足して母指拳 ＊　気合
94–Yori–Ashi and Bosiken–Zuki ＊ Kiai

95―寄り足で下がる。引手構え
95–Return by Yori–Ashi, doing Hikite and Kamae

96―平行立ちに戻る
96–Return to Heiko–Dachi

97―結び立ち。両のかかとを同時に引き合わせる
97–Musubi–Dachi by ataching both heel

98―礼
98–Rei

十六（セイリュウ）の形は上地流二世の上地完英先生が創作した。

十三の形は有段者へのレベルに到達した事を意味するのに対し、十六の形は、その後さらに精進を重ねてゆく段階を意味している。

Sanseiryu was created by Kanei Uchi, the Second Generation Master of Uechi–Ryu.

Seisan(13 years old) means the arrival at black belt, and Seiryu (16 years old) means the necessity of training for self–development after becoming an adult(black belt).

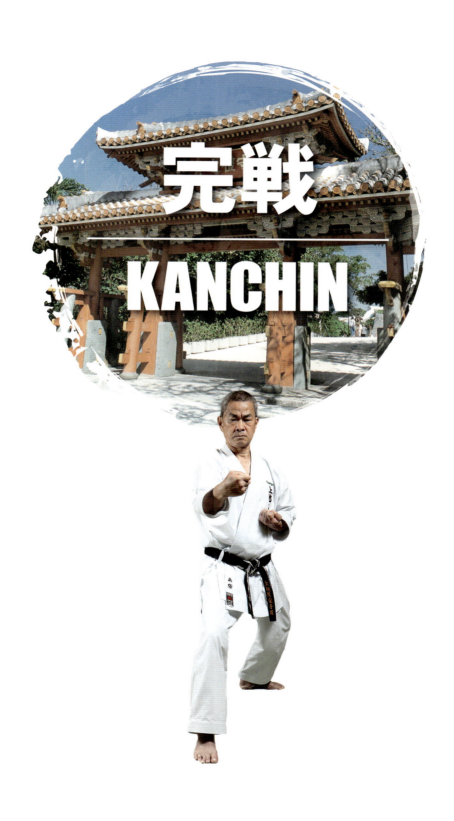

完戦
KANCHIN

完戦（カンチン）KANCHIN

向正面から見た写真
The pictures shown from the back front

＊印は極めを入れる
＊ Sign of impact

1—結び立ち
1–Musubi–Dachi

2—礼
2–Rei

3—「用意」の準備、三戦と同じ動き
3–Prepare "Yooi" as Sanchin

4—「用意」、三戦と同じ動き
4–"Yooi" in same way as Sanchin

5—右足を踏み出し、平手構え
5–Slide forward right foot, Kamae

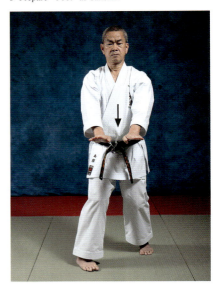
6—上段手甲拳受けに移る
6–Begin Jodan Shuko–Ken–Uke

7—上段縦手甲拳受け
7–Vertical Jodan Shuko–Ken–Uke

8—中段縦掌低受けに移る
8–Begin vertical Chudan Shotei–Uke

9—中段縦掌低受け
9–Vertical Chudan Shotei–Uke

10－中段横手甲拳受け
10–Horizontal Chudan Shuko–Ken–Uke

11－内側への掌低
11–Shotei–Uke to inside

12－左へ90°転進、右前足を移動
12–Turn to left side 90° moving front foot

13－三戦立ち、正面から見た図
13–Sanchi–Dachi and Kamae

14－左手の平手廻し受け
14–Begin Hirate–Mawashi–Uke of left hand

15－左手の平手廻し受け ＊
15–Hirate–Mawashi–Uke of left hand ＊

16－右前足で正面蹴り ＊
16–Mae–Geri of right front foot ＊

17－引き足
17–Hiki–Ashi

18－三戦立ちで構え
18–Return to Sanchin–Dachi, Kamae

19－右前足を右側90°へ移して真後ろへ転進
19–Move right front to side 90° to face to back

20－次に後足を移して真後ろに向かう、三戦立ち
20–And move back foot, Sancin–Dachi

21－真後ろに回転した20図を向正面から見る
21–Front view of Picture 20, after turning to back

22－左手の平手廻し受けに移る
22–Prepare Hirate–Mawashi–Uke of left hand

23－左手の平手廻し受け ＊
23–Hirate–Mawashi–Uke of left hand ＊

24－左後足の前蹴り ＊
24–Mae–Geri of left back foot ＊

25－引き足
25–Hiki–Ashi

26－三戦立ちで構え
26–Sanchin–Dachi, Kamae

27－膝受け、輪受けに移る （27-29図は一連の動作）
27–Begin Hiza–Uke and Wa–Uke
(Pictures 27-29 are serial actions)

28—膝受け、輪受けを同時に行う ＊
28—Do Hiza–Uke and Wa–Uke at same time ＊

29—猫足立ちで構え ＊ 27～29図を同時に行う
29—Neko–Ashi–Dachi and Kamae ＊ Do Picture 27-29 at the same time

30—縦肘突きに移る
30—Begin Tate–Hiji–Zuki

31—左後足を大きく踏み込む、左手の平手廻し受けに移る
31—Do a long slide step with left back foot and begin Hirate–Mawashi–Uke of left hand

32—さらに右後足を大きく踏み込み、前屈立ちで、平手廻し受け
32—Take a Zenkutsu–Dachi with a long slide step of right foot and Hirate–Mawashi–Uke

33—縦肘突き、前屈立ち ＊ 気合！
33—Tate–Hiji–Zuki on Zenkutsu–Dachi ＊ Kiai！

34—後屈立ちになり、すくい受けに移る
34—Return to Kokutsu–Dachi and begin Shoken–Sukui–Uke

35—平手廻し受けの要領で小拳すくい受けをする
35—Do Shoken–Sukui–Uke in same way of Hirate–Mawashi–Uke

36—小拳すくい受け ＊
36—Shoken–Sukui–Uke and Kamae ＊

37ー小拳すくいはね上げ ＊
37–Shoken–Sukui Hane–Age(throw up out) ＊

38ー引き手で構える
38–Hikite and Kamae

39ー左90°へ転進、右足を軸軸に回転。膝受け、すくい受け
39–Turn to left 90° on front of left front foot with Hiza–Uke and Sukui–Uke

40ー膝受け、下段払い、すくい受けを同時に行う事
40–Do at same time Hiza–Uke, Gedan–Barai and Sukui–Uke

41ー膝受け、下段払い、すくい受けが同時に終わり、猫足立ち ＊
41–Finish three actions at same time and Neko–Ashi–Dachi ＊

42ー41図を正面側から見る
42–Left side view of Picture 41

43ー真正面への転進、左前足を移動させる
43–Return to front by moving left front foot to front side

44ー後足を軸に左前足を移す
44–Face to front on the spot with Sanchin–Kamae

45ー鯉の尻尾打ち、左から開始
45–Koi-no-Shippo-Uchi(Shukou-Ken and Shotei), begin from left side

46−右へ2回目
46–2nd action to right side

47−左へ3回目
47–3rd action to left side

48−右で4回目、極めを入れ、止める ＊
48–4th time to right side, stop with Kime(Impact) ＊

49−前方45°右へ向かい、上げ受けへ移る。三戦立ち
49–Turn at 45° to front right side corner by Sanchin–Dachi. Begin Age–Uke

50−諸手の上げ受け ＊
50–Morote Age–Uke(Both hands Age–Uke) facing to 45°corner ＊

51−右前足を大きく踏み込みながら挟み受けに移る
51–Begin Hasami–Uke with a long slide step of right front foot to 45°

52−後屈立ちで挟み受け ＊
52–Hasami–Uke on Kokutsu–Dachi ＊

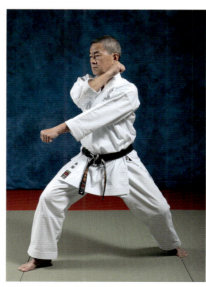

53−正拳の下段払いに移る
53–Begin Seiken Gedan–Barai

54−正拳下段払い ＊
54–Seiken–Gedan–Barai ＊

87

55－小拳すくい受けに移る
55–Begin Shoken–Sukui–Uke

56－内小手で絡める
56–Sweep by arm inside

57－肘を軸に拳を返す ✱
57–On the axis of elbow, scoop of Mawashi–Uke with Shoken ✱

58－すくって、はね上げる ✱
58–Scoop up, throw out forearm ✱

59－引き手にして構える
59–Hikite and Kamae

60－左真横に回転、体をひねり、右前足を後ろに移す
60–Turn to left side on front of left back foot by moving front foot to behind

61－左真横に小拳で三戦立ち
61–Sanchi–Dachi and Kamae with Shoken of both hands

62－小拳突きに移る
62–Begin Shoken–Zuki of right hand

63－1回目の小拳突き、その場で行う
63–1st Shoken–Zuki on the spot with ritht hand

64ー中段の小拳突き
64–Full Chudan Shoken–Zuki

65ー引き手で構える
65–Hikite and Kamae

66ー2回目の小拳突き、寄り足しながら拳を引く
66–Begin 2nd Shoken–Zuki with Yori–Ashi

67ー寄り足しながら引き手
67–Pull back hand by doing Yori–Ashi

68ー止まった時点で突く ✱
68–Shoken–Zuki at point of stop ✱

69ー3回目の小拳突き ✱ 66ー68図と同じ要領で行う。但し、最後に三戦構えに戻る
69–Do 3rd Shoken–Zuki ✱ in same way as Picture 66–68, Sanchin–Kamae

70ー小拳突きの後、引き手で構える
70–After 3rd Shoken–Zuki, Hirate and Shoken–Kamae with Sanchin–Dachi

71ー小拳すくい受けに移る
71–Begin Shoken–Sukui–Uke

72ー後屈立ちで小拳すくい受け、55-59図の要領で行う
72–Koukutsu–Dachi and Shoken–Sukui–Uke, Do it in same way of Picture 55-59

73―小拳すくい受け、後屈立ち ＊
73–Shoken–Sukui–Uke ＊

74―小拳はね上げ ＊
74–Hane–Age (throw out forearm) ＊

75―引き手にし、構える
75–Hikite and Kamae

76―右へ180°回転する。右前足のつま先軸に体をひねり、反対に向く
76–Turn to right side. Turn the body on front of both feet to right side(180°)

77―右足で滑り込み、後屈立ち、平手廻し受けに移る
77–Do a long slide step of right foot for Koukutsu–Dachi and do Hirate–Mawashi–Uke

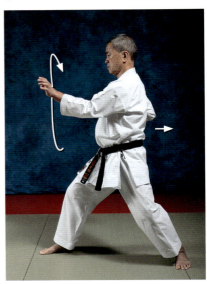

78―滑り込みながら平手廻し受けをし、横振り肘に移る ＊
78–Hirate–Mawashi–Uke on Koukutusu–Dachi for Yoko–Furi–Hiji ＊

79―横振り肘 ＊ 気合！
79–Yoko–Furi–Hiji ＊ Kiai !

80―縦裏拳打ち ＊
80–Tate–Uraken–Uchi ＊

81―右手を引き、小拳突きに移る
81–Pull back right hand for Shoken–Zuki

82－中段小拳突き ✱
82–Chudan–Shoken–Zuki ✱

83－正面へ向かう。左足のつま先を軸に転進する。三戦構え
83–Turn to front on front of left foot. Sanchin–Dachi and Kamae

84－三戦抜き手に移る
84–Begin Sanchin–Nukite

85－脇に引き手
85–Pull back right hand to chest

86－三戦抜き手 ✱
86–Sanchin–Nukite ✱

87－引き手で三戦構え
87–Hikite and Sanchin–Kamae

88－渡り受けに移る
88–Begin Watari–Uke with right hand

89－右手で大きく平手廻し受け ✱
89–Usual Hirate–Mawashi–Uke of right hand and do a small one with left hand ✱

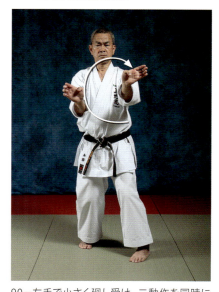

90－左手で小さく廻し受け。二動作を同時に終わらせること
90–✱ Do a small Hirate–Mawashi–Uke of left hand. Finish two actions at same time

91－小拳押え突きに移る
91–Prepare Shoken–Osae–Zuki

92－寄り足しながら押さえる ✽
92–Osae–Uke with Yori–Ashi ✽

93－中段小拳突き ✽ 気合！
93–Chudan Shoken–Zuki ✽ Kiai !

94－寄り足で後ろへ下りながら、両手を小拳にして重ねる
94–Yori–Ashi back and Kamae with Shoken of both hands as Kanshiwa

95－小拳構え、小拳の甲を重ねて構える。平行立ちになる
95–Shoken–Kamae and Heikou–Dachi

96－両足のかかとを同時に引いて、結び立ち
96–Join both heels for Musubi–Dachi

97－礼
97–Rei

補足説明カット

●61〜64図、66〜75図について補足する説明カットを掲載する。
●Supplementary explanation about Picture 61-64, 66-75.

小拳突きと小拳すくい受け
Shoken–Zuki and Shoken Sukui–Uke

61図、小拳構え、三戦立ち
Picture 61: Sanchin–Dachi and Shoken Kamae

62図、一回目はその場で小拳突き
Picture 62: 1st Shoken–Zuki on the place

63図、三戦抜き手の要領で引き手
Picture 63: Pull back Shoken as Sanchin–Nukite

64図ー中段小拳突き ＊
Picture 64:Chudan–Shoken–Zuki ＊ and Hikite

66図ー2回目の小拳突き、寄り足しながら小拳を引く
Picture 66:2nd Shoken–Zuki. Pull back right hand to chest side by doing Yori–Ashi

67図ー脇に引く、寄り足しながら同時に行う
Picture 67:Hikite and Yori–Ashi at the same time

68図、止まった時点で小拳突き ＊
Picture 68:Do Shoken–Zuki at point of stop ＊

69図、3回目の小拳突きに移る
Picture 69:Begin 3rd Shoken–Zuki by doing Yori–Ashi

69図、2回目と同じ要領で行なう
Picture 69:Do in the same way as 2nd one

69図、3回目の小拳突き ＊
Picture 69:3rd Shoken–Zuki ＊

70図、引き手で小拳構え
Picture 70:Hikite and Shoken–Kamae

71図、小拳すくい受けに移る
Picture 71:Begin Shoken–Sukui–Uke

72図、後足を滑り込ませ、後屈立ち。前腕を絡ませるようにし、肘を軸に拳を返す
Picture 72:Take Kokutsu–Dachi by sliding right back foot forward and begin Shoken–Sukui–Uke

73図、小拳すくい受け ＊
Picture 73:Shoken–Sukui–Uke ＊ Do Shoken Sukui–Uke same as small Hirate–Mawashi–Uke with Shoken

74図、小拳ではね上げる ＊
Picture 74:Throw up forearm in the air ＊

75図、引き手にして構える
Picture 75:Hikite and Kamae

完戦（カンチン）も上地流二世の上地完英先生の創作。上地流開祖の完文を追慕して創作した。完文の戦い―完文であれば、このような技法を駆使して戦うであろうとの思いをこめて、この形を創作し、さらには、この形の段階まで来ると、完全に独り立ちして、難局を乗り越えていける技量を意味している。

Kanchin was also created by Kanei Uechi, the Second Generation of Uechi–Ryu, to cherish the memory of Kanbun Uechi, the Founder of this style.

Kanchin means the battle of Kanbun and also signifies that the technical ability is obtained to individually deal with any difficult situation when arriving at this level of Kata.

三十六（サンセイリュウ）SANSEIRYU

向正面から見た写真
The pictures shown from the back front
＊ 印は極めを入れる
＊ Sign of impact

1－結び立ち
1–Musubi–Dachi

2－礼
2–Rei

3－結び立ち
3–Musubi–Dachi

4－「用意」の初動、拳を腰に引きながら、両つま先をわずかに開く
4–Begin "Yooi". Pull up both hands to the waist, slightly open the front of both feet

5－「用意」、拳を丸く下げながら、両かかとを同時に開く、平行立ち
5–"Yooi", circularly get down both hands and open both heels at the same time, Heikou–Dachi

6－左足を踏み出し、構える、三戦立ち
6–Slide left foot, open both hands, Sanchi–Dachi, Kamae

7－渡り受けに移る
7–Bigin Watari–Uke with right hand

8－初めに右手で通常の平手廻し受け ＊
8–1st usual Hirate–Mawashi–Uke of right hand ＊

9－次に左手で小さく平手廻し受けをする。ただし、二動作は同時に終わらせること
9–2nd small Hirate–Mawashi–Uke of left hand, the two actions should be finished at the same time ＊

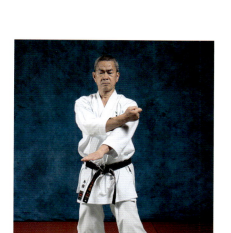
10ー小拳押さえ突きに移る
10–Begin Shoken–Osae–Zuki

11ー寄り足しながら押さえる ＊
11–Osae–Uke with Yori–Ashi forward ＊

12ー止まった時点で突く ＊
12–Shoken–Zuki at point of stop ＊

13ー寄り足で下がり、両手の小拳の甲を重ねて、構える
13–Yori–Ashi back and Shoken Kamae as Kanshiwa

14ー真後ろへ180°回転、後足のつま先を軸に踵を廻して回転
14–Turn to backward(180°) as Sanchin–Turn

15ー真後ろの図を正面に見る。三戦立ちで小拳の構え
15–Front view of back. Shoken Kamae on Sanchin–Dachi

16ー縦肘突きに移る
16–Begin Tate–Hiji–Zuki

17ー前屈立ちで踏み込みながら平手廻し受けをする ＊
17–Hirate–Mawashi–Uke by stepping inside for Zenkutsu–Dachi ＊

18ー着地の時点で縦肘突き ＊　気合！
18–Tate–Hiji–Zuki after Mawashi–Uke at point of landing ＊ Kiai !

SANSEIRYU

19―三戦立ちに戻り、母指拳突きに移る
19–Return to Sanchin–Dachi and begin Boshi-ken–Zuki

20―右手の平手廻し受け ✻
20–Hirate–Mawashi–Uke of right hand

21―左手で上段母指拳突き ✻
21–Jodan Boshiken–Zuki of left hand ✻

22―四本抜き手に移る
22–Begin Yonhon–Nukite

23―左手の平手廻し受け ✻
23–Hirate–Mawashi–Uke of left hand ✻

24―四本抜き手 ✻
24–Yonhon–Nukite of right hand ✻

25―引き手で構える
25–Hikite and Kamae

26―正面へ180°回転、三戦の要領で回転する
26–Return to front 180° as Sanchin–Turn

27―正面図、三戦立ちで構える
27–Front view, Sanchin–Dachi and Kamae

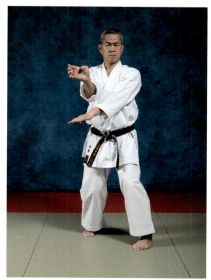

28－前足正面蹴りに移る
28–Begin Mae–Geri of left front foot

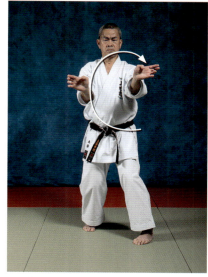

29－左手の平手廻し受け ✱
29–Hirate–Mawashi–Uke of left hand ✱

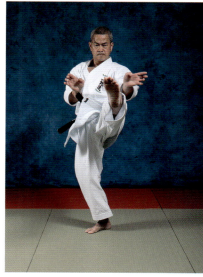

30－左前足の正面蹴り ✱
30–Mae–Geri of left front foot ✱

31－引き足で構える
31–Hiki–Ashi and Kamae

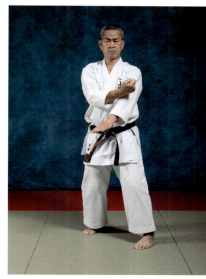

32－小拳での押え突きに移る
32–Begin Shoken–Osae–Zuki

33－寄り足で進みながら押さえる。小拳を脇に引く
33–Yori–Ashi forward and Osae–Uke of left hand, pull back right hand to the chest

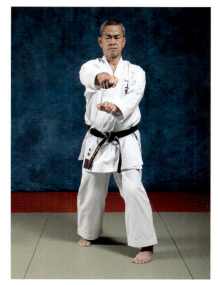

34－小拳突き ✱
34–Shoken–Zuki ✱

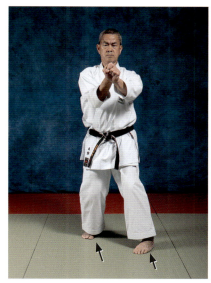

35－寄り足で下がりながら小拳で構える。小拳の甲を重ねる
35–Yori–Ashi back and Shoken Kamae as Kanshiwa

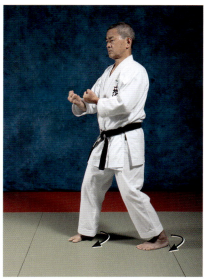

36－正面右45°への上げ受けに移る。両つま先を軸に右角へ向う
36–Begin Age–Uke of both hands by facing to right 45°of the front. Change the direcion on the spot with Sanchin–Dachi

37ー諸手の上段上げ受け ✳
37–Morote–Jodan–Age–Uke(both hands Age–Uke) ✳

38ー正面左45°へ転進、膝受けと下段払い、すくい受けに移る
38–Change the direction to left side 45° of front on the spot. Begin left foot Hiza–Uke, left hand Gedan–Barai, right hand Sukui–Uke

39ー正面左45°方向へ、猫足立ちで構える。✳ 三動作を同時に行う
39–Finish three actions at same time and Neko–Ashi–Dachi Kamae to 45° of left side of the front ✳

40ー左真横へ向かう。前足を移して転進し、三戦立ちで構える
40–Turn to full left side by moving left front foot. Sanchi–Kamae

41ー正面左45°へ転進、前足つま先を軸に向きを変える。後ろ足で進む
41–Return to 45° left side. Slide back foot on front of the front foot

42ー後ろ足で踏み込んで後屈立ち、両平手ではさみ倒す ✳
42–Slide a long step of back foot for Kokutsu–Dachi and do Hirate–Hasami–Uke of both hands ✳

43ーその場で正拳下段払いに移る
43–Begin Seiken–Gedan–Barai on the spot

44ー正拳下段払い ✳
44–Seiken–Gedan–Barai ✳

45ー次に小拳すくい受けに移る
45–Begin Shoken–Sukui–Uke on the spot

46－内小手で内払いにし、肘を軸に拳を返す
46–Sweep arm inside and turn Shoken on axis of elbow

47－小拳すくい受け ✽
47–Shoken–Sukui–Uke ✽

48－跳ね上げる。その後、引き手にして47図の姿勢に戻る ✽
48–Throw up and pull back arms to return to the stance of Picture 47 ✽

49－後足を軸に、後方左45°に回転する
49–Turn to left side 45° of the back on front of back left foot

50－両手を小拳にして三戦立ちの姿勢を取る
50–Sanchin–Dachi with Shoken–Kamae of both hands

51－その場で、右小拳突きに移る
51–Begin Shoken–Zuki of right hand on the spot

52－脇に右小拳を引く
52–Pull back right hand to chest

53－その場で小拳突き ✽
53–Shoken–Zuki on the spot ✽

54－2回目の小拳突きに移る
54–Begin 2nd Shoken–Zuki

101

SANSEIRYU

55―寄足で進み、右小拳を引く
55–Slide forward by Yori-Ashi of both feet, Hikite (pull back right Shoken)

56―止まった時点で小拳突き ✱
56–Shoken-Zuki at point of stop Yori-Ashi ✱

57―3回目の小拳突きに移る
57–Begin 3rd Shoken-Zuki

58―寄足進みながら拳を引く
58–Pull back Shoken on Yori-Ashi

59―止まった時点で小拳突き ✱
59–Shoken-Zuki at point of stop Yori-Ashi ✱

60―小拳すくい受けに移る
60–Hikite, and begin Shoken-Sukui-Uke by sliding for Kokutsu-Dachi

61―後足で踏み込んで後屈立ち
61–Long slide step of back foot for Kokutsu-Dachi. Do Uchi-barai of inside arm of right hand

62―内小手で内払いし、肘を軸に小拳を返す
62–After Uchi-Barai, do Mawashi-Ueke of Shoken on the axis of elbow

63―小拳すくい受け ✱
63–Shoken-Sukui-Uke and Kamae ✱

64－小拳はね上げ ＊
64–Shoken–Hane–Age(throw forearm up) ＊

65－小拳すくい受けの構えに戻る
65–Return to Shoken–Sukui–Uke Kamae

66－正面へ回転し横振り肘に移る。後足のつま先を軸に回転
66–Return to front by a long slide step on front of back foot for Kokutsu–Dachi to perform Yoko–Furi–Hiji

67－後足で踏み込みながら、左手で平手廻し受けをする。後屈立ちを取る
67–Slide back foot for Kokutsu–Dachi and do Hirate–Mawashi–Uke of left hand

68－平手廻し受け ＊
68–Hirate–Mashi–Uke by sliding for Kokutsu–Dachi ＊

69－横振り肘 ＊　気合！
69–Yoko–Furi–Hiji and Kiai! ＊

70－縦裏拳打ち ＊
70–Tate–Uraken–Uchi ＊

71－脇に小拳を引く
71–Pull back to chest side

72－小拳突き ＊
72–Shoken–Zuki ＊

SANSEIRYU

73－後ろ左45°へ回転、後足のつま先を軸に腰をひねって向く
73–Turn to left back corner45°(from front side) on back foot by twisting the waist

74－右後足を大きく踏み込む、前屈立ちになりながら、左手の平手廻し受け
74–Slide a long step for Zenkutsu–Dachi by doing Hirate–Mawasi–Uke of left hand

75－左手の平手廻し受け、右手は脇に引き、縦肘の準備 ＊
75–Hirate–Mawashi–Uke of left hand and pull back rght hand to chest for Tate–Hiji ＊

76－平手廻し受けが終わった時点で縦肘突き ＊ 気合！
76–After Hirate–Mawashi–Uke, vertical right Tate–Hiji–Zuki ＊ Kiai !

77－後屈立ちになり、小拳すくい受けに移る
77–Return to Kokutsu–Dachi and begin Shoken–Sukui–Uke

78－内小手で内払いし、肘を軸に小拳を返す
78–Sweep by inside of right arm and turn Shoken on axis of elbow

79－小拳すくい受け ＊
79–Shoken–Sukui–Uke as Mawashi–Uke ＊

80－小拳ではね上げ、構えに戻る
80–Shoken–Hane–Age, Hikite and Kamae

81－正面に向きを変える
81–Return to front

82―正面に向かい、三戦構え
82–Return to front, Sanchin–Kamae

83―三戦抜き手に移る
83–Begin Sanchin–Nukite

84―脇に引き手
84–Pull back right hand to chest

85―三戦抜き手 ✱
85–Full Sanchin–Nukite ✱

86―引き手にして、三戦構え
86–Hikite and Sanchin–Kamae

87―左真横に転進、左前足を左に移し、後足のつま先を軸にかかとをひねる
87–Turn to left side by moving left front foot on axis of front of back foot

88―三戦構えをする
88–Sanchin–Dachi and Kamae

89―膝受け、輪受けに移る
89–Begin Hiza–Uke and Wa–Uke

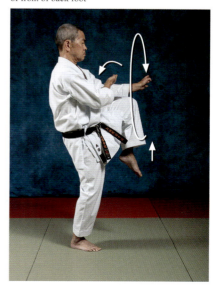

90―膝受けと輪受けを同時に行う
90–Begin Hiza–Uke and Wa–Uke at same time

SANSEIRYU

91-猫足立ちで構える。89〜91図を同時に行う
91–Finish Hiza-Uke /Wa-Uke at same time. Kamae on Neko-Ashi-Dachi

92-三戦立ちに戻り、構える
92–Return to Sanchi-Dachi for turning

93-右反対に回転。三戦と同じ要領で後ろへ回転
93–Turn to right side as Sanchin-Turn

94-膝受けと輪受けを同時に行う
94–Do Hiza-Uke and Wa-Uke at the same time

95-二動作を同時に終了して、猫足立ちで構える
95–Finish two actions at the same time and Kamae on Neko-Ashi-Dachi

96-正面に向かう。三戦立ち
96–Turn to front on the spot and Sanchin-Dachi

97-平手廻し受けと鶴嘴拳（かくしけん）に移る
97–Begin Hirate-Mawashi-Uke and Kakushi-Ken with Sanchin-Step forward

98-後足を踏み込みながら、平手廻し受けをし、鶴嘴拳を振り上げる
98–Sanchin-Step, Hirate-Mawashi-Uke and pull up Kakushi-Ken. Perform three actions at the same time

99-踏み込んだ時点で、鶴嘴拳を打つ ＊ 気合！三戦立ちを保つ
99–Stab with Kakushi-Ken at the same time as step-in ＊ Kiai! Keep Sanchin-Dachi

100―鶴嘴拳を打った後で、引き手
100–After Kakushi–Ken, Hikite and Kamae

101―前足を引いて下がる。後足は膝受けの姿勢。左手の平手廻し受け
101–Step back by pulling back right front foot and do Hiza–Uke/Hirate–Mawashi–Uke of left hand

102―平手廻し受けと膝の下しを同時に行う。猫足立ちとなる
102–Finish Hiza–Uke, Hirate–Mawashi–Uke at same time. Neko–Ashi–Dachi

103―平行立ちに戻る
103–Return to Hiekou–Dachi

104―結び立ち、両かかとを同時に合わせる
104–Return to Musubi–Dachi. Bring both heels together at the same time

105―礼
105–Rei

　三十六（サンセイリュウ）は中国福建省から上地完文により導入された。上地流の八つの形の最後の形であり、最高峰の形である。

　上地完文は中国福建省に1897年から1910年まで13年間滞在し、師父の周子和からパンガイヌーン拳法を習い、三戦、十三、三十六の三つの形を沖縄に持ち帰った。この三つの形に完子和、完周、十戦、十六、完戦の五つを加えた計八つの形があくまでも上地流の正統な形である。

形の名前と順序 (The name of Katas and the order of learning)
1) 三戦（サンチン）Sanchin
2) 完子和（カンシワ）Kanshiwa
3) 完周（カンシュウ）Kanshu
4) 十戦（セイチン）Seichin
5) 十三（セイサン）Seisan
6) 十六（セイリュウ）Seiryu
7) 完戦（カンチン）Kanchin
8) 三十六（サンセイリュウ）Sanseiryu

Sanseiryu was introduced by Kanbun Uechi directly from Fujian, China, which is the last and highest Kata of eight Uechi–Ryu Katas. Kanbun Uechi stayed in Fujian, China for 13 years from 1897 to 1910.

He learned Pangainoon style boxing from Shu Shiwa(Zhou Zihe in Chinese) and brought back three Katas of Sanchin, Seisan and Sanseiryu to Okinawa.

Incluing these three Katas, Kanshiwa, Kanshu, Seichin, Seiryu and Kanchin, there are eight Katas in Uechi–ryu which are being taught as the authentic Katas since the time of Kanei Uechi, the Second Generation Master and the father of the restoration of Uechi–Ryu.

終わりに

　太平洋戦争が終わって間もない頃、1950年代の話である。沖縄には戦前の風習がまだ色濃く残っていた。沖縄の少年達は、15、16歳になると巻きわらを突いていた。家の庭の片隅に、自分用の巻きわらを立て、学校帰りに友達と一緒に突いていた。

　これは沖縄的な風習であったかも知れない。少年達は恐らく、皆強い男になりたかったのであろう。心身の鍛錬を目的に少年達は空手に大きな関心を持っていた。男は皆空手をやる。それが沖縄の少年達が引き継いだ血であったのであろう。

　空手道は身体の鍛錬から入り、精神力を強化し、人格を磨き上げる大きな教育効果を持っている。体育と徳育の両面を持ち合わせた、自己確立という人間教育の特徴が顕著である。

　空手道が競技化されて久しい。とはいえ、それは1970年代に入ってからである。競技化は空手道の一局面に過ぎない。競技生活の寿命は短い。他方、武道の修業は終生続く。死ぬまで心身の鍛錬は続くのである。「技より入って、道に進め」とは先達の言葉である。

　空手道はあくまでも、技術と精神の両面において完成された一つの武道である。修業者は、特に空手道の精神と伝統的な技に誠実に向き合わねばならない。誠実な取り組みが健全な空手道の普及発展につながるのである。

　なお、本書の出版における編集作業では、雑誌『モモト』編集室のいのうえちず氏にご尽力いただき、編集工房 東洋企画の皆さんにも多大なご協力を賜りました。この場を借りて、心からのお礼を申し上げます。

2017年6月吉日
上地流空手道協会欧州支部代表
範士九段　島袋　幸信

Post script

筆者、鶴嘴拳（かくしけん）、2007年
Y. Shimabukuro, Kakushi–Ken、2007

For several years after the World War Ⅱ, in the year of 1950, many old customs which came from the old Okinawa, were seen around us.

The Okinawan boys, when they were 15 or 16 years old, were hitting the Makiwara made in the garden.

It certainly seemed a special Okinawan custom. The boys probably wanted to become strong men.

They were especially interested in Karate for the purpose of training the body and the spirit. All the boys had to practice Karate without exception. That was probably a special culture passed on to the Okinawan boys from generation to generation.

Karate–Do which begins with physical training has a big educative effect to enforce the mental power and to build up the character. Having two sides of physical and moral education, Karate–Do has a remarkable effect on the human education.

Although many decades have passed since the competition of Karate–Do started, it only became popular after the 1970's. The competition is only one phase of Karate–Do, and the life of athletes is not so long. On the other hand, the practice of martial arts continues until the end of one's life. The physical and mental training continues until death like the eternal self–education.

Karate–Do is a martial art without doubt, being a complete martial art on the two phases of the technique and the spirit. The practitioners must face its traditional technique and its spirit with a sincere attitude. The sincere engagement to Karate–Do shall bring a wholesome diffusion and development of this discipline.

The pioneers said, "Begin from the technique, and go forward to the way. " I am sure that Karate–Do gives us a physical and spiritual beauty and helps us to finish our life peacefully.

Yukinobu SHIMABUKURO, Hanshi 9 Dan
Representative of Uechi-Ryu Karate-Do Kyokai in Europe

著者近影

著者プロフィール
島袋幸信（しまぶくろ　ゆきのぶ）
1942年生まれ、沖縄県浦添市内間出身。
1962年に上地流空手道について當山清幸師範に師事。
以降、上原勇、上地完英、上地完明各師範に師事。
1984年7月再渡仏し以降定住。フランス、ベルギー、スロベニア、スペイン、ポーランド、ロシア等で上地流空手道を指導。
2007年8月に上地流宗家より九段を允許(いんきょ)され、宗家系上地流の欧州代表に委託された。

Author Profil
Yukinobu Shimabukuro (1942-), author of this book, learned Uechi-Ryu with Seiko Toyama, Isamu Uehara in Tokyo, Kanei Uechi and Kanmei Uechi. He has been living and teaching Uechi-Ryu in France since 1984. He has received his 9 Dan in 2007 from Uechi-Ryu Soke, and nominated Representative of Uechi-Ryu Soke in Europe. The Soke group in France has now expanded into 15 dojos with about 500 practitioners and also into other European countries such as Spain, Belgium, Poland and Russia.

郵便振替　01780-3-58425

※無断複写・複製・転載を禁じます。

上地流空手道 ―写真と解説で見る上地流の形―

2017年7月1日　第1版発行

著　者　島袋幸信
発 行 者　大城　孝
発 行 所　編集工房 東洋企画
　　　　　〒901-0306
　　　　　沖縄県糸満市西崎町4丁目21-5
　　　　　TEL：098-995-4444　FAX：098-995-4448
　　　　　[E-mail] info@toyo-plan.co.jp
　　　　　[URL] https://toyo-plan.co.jp
印　刷　株式会社 東洋企画印刷
製　本　沖縄製本株式会社

ISBN978-4-905412-74-8 C3375 ¥1500
郵便振替　01780-3-58425
C2016　Toyo Plan Printed in Japan
※無断複写・複製・転載を禁じます。
※乱丁・落丁の場合は、お取り替えいたします。